GW00394043

Is the BBC in ᵣₑᵣₕ.

Does It Deserve to Be?

Edited by

John Mair and Tom Bradshaw

The right of John Mair and Tom Bradshaw to be identified as the authors and editors of this work has been asserted by them in accordance with the Copyright, Design and Patents Act 1988

Cover Design Dean Stockton

Published by Bite-Sized Books Ltd 2020

Bite-Sized Books Ltd Cleeve Croft, Cleeve Road, Goring RG8 9BJ UK
information@bite-sizedbooks.com
Registered in the UK. Company Registration No: 9395379
ISBN: 9798617963573

Contents

Acknowledgments

This book is timely by design. Since the December 2019 General Election the Boris Johnson Government and the Prime Minister's chief adviser, Dominic Cummings, have made it clear that they have the BBC in their crosshairs. While "crisis" is a word that is frequently used in connection with the corporation, it is not exaggerating to say that this one is very serious; existential, even.

As a former BBC producer, I declare my (not uncritical) interest in seeing the continuation of this great national institution. I think it is a force for huge good and have edited two previous books on this subject, *Is the BBC in Crisis?* (Abramis, 2014) and *The BBC Today: Future Uncertain* (Abramis, 2015). I care about the debate.

In order to inform and stimulate a vital national debate, this book was curated in record time. Ten weeks from idea to reality between covers. That could not have been achieved without the work and efficiency of our twenty (unpaid) authors, the brilliant cover designer Dean Stockton and our publisher Paul Davies.

We owe them all huge gratitude.

John Mair, Oxford
with Tom Bradshaw, Cheltenham

The Editors

Tom Bradshaw studied philosophy at the University of Cambridge and now combines academic posts with a career as a freelance sports writer and broadcaster. He has written for national titles across South Africa and the UK, including *The Times, The Guardian* and *Times Literary Supplement*. He is a regular co-commentator and pundit for the BBC's rugby coverage. He is senior lecturer in the School of Media at the University of Gloucestershire in Cheltenham, and earlier this year published, with Daragh Minogue, *Sports Journalism: The State of Play* (Routledge, 2020). His research focuses on media ethics and in 2018 he guest edited an issue of *The International Journal of Communication Ethics* that focused on ethical issues affecting sports journalism. He has published numerous papers and articles on media law, pedagogy and philosophy.

John Mair has taught journalism at the Universities of Coventry, Kent, Northampton, Brunel, Edinburgh Napier, Guyana and the Communication University of China. He has edited 28 'hackademic' volumes over the last eight years on subjects ranging from trust in television, the health of investigative journalism, reporting the 'Arab Spring', to three volumes on the Leveson Inquiry. John also created the Coventry Conversations, which attracted 350 media movers and shakers to Coventry University. Since then, he has launched the Northampton Chronicles, Media Mondays at Napier and most recently the Harrow Conversations at Westminster University. In a previous life, he was an award-winning producer/director for the BBC, ITV and Channel 4, and a secondary school teacher.

Foreword

The BBC and the dispassionate interrogation of those in power

The BBC is an arm of the people and not an arm of government, says Peter Snow. And long may that continue

I was mighty glad to hear Boris Johnson say in the Commons recently that he agreed the BBC was "a cherished British institution". I'm sure most British people would say so too. And even if fewer young people watch the BBC these days I'm sure they're all glad it's there. To undermine, let alone destroy, a broadcasting system that is the envy of the world and which gives advertisement-free programming with universal appeal would be an act of mindless self-harm. So what problem do some people have with the BBC?

Impenetrable decision-making

True, it's not free. It costs each viewer £3 a week. But that's a lot less than the cost to us consumers of the amount advertising contributes to prices in the shops. And to argue that the BBC can be funded by subscription like Netflix is a flawed comparison. Netflix provides pure entertainment, not the rich combination of news, education and features that is public service broadcasting.

It is certainly true that the BBC's management is absurdly bloated and its decision-making process a jungle of almost impenetrable complexity. It has been rightly ridiculed by the BBC's own producers in the programme *W1A*. People have been shouting for a drastic reduction of the bureaucracy for decades. That is a must and the current row is a perfect opportunity for action.

The BBC also comes under attack from all directions for what people imagine is some kind of political bias. Maddeningly, there are people in politics and other positions of power who believe exactly that. It is shameful that many of those who resent close scrutiny from the BBC attempt to denigrate it by claiming TV and radio broadcasters are somehow being leant on. It's nonsense.

No one to my knowledge has ever actually demonstrated that anyone in BBC News or current affairs management has directed that there should be some kind of deliberate campaign to damage a political party or government. Anyone even airing the idea would have been laughed out of court.

Pride in independence

I have spent a lifetime covering public events at ITN and the BBC, reporting political affairs as newscaster, diplomatic and defence correspondent at ITN, anchoring Newsnight at the BBC and presenting election programmes on both. We were all proud of that 'I' in ITN. 'Independent' was the watchword that inspired our reporting, and I found all my colleagues at the BBC no less fiercely proud of their independence. And that dispassionate determination not to discredit but to interrogate those in power is still vigorously alive. Indeed if anything people are disappointed that this drive to expose hypocrisy and get at the truth has not been pressed harder amid all the ups and downs of the last three years.

The BBC, just like ITN, is not an arm of government. The BBC is an arm of the people. The job of BBC journalists – reporters, writers and interviewers – is to reveal what people are entitled to know about the way business, government and public affairs are run. Long may they continue to do so, with even more vigour.

About the contributor

Peter Snow is a broadcaster, journalist and presenter who has covered some of the pivotal moments of recent British political history. He presented Newsnight for almost two decades following its launch in 1980, and has frequently appeared as an analyst of general election results. He has also published a number of history books.

Introduction

Tom Bradshaw

It seems there are more questions about the BBC today than there are questions on *Question Time*. Is the licence fee sustainable in its current form, and should those who avoid paying it really go before the courts? Has the corporation been superseded by technology that makes subscription a more obvious model for media consumption? Is its long-vaunted impartiality intact, or even achievable? Has it over-reached itself by trying to do too much in too many spheres of media? In a post-Brexit landscape, how important is the BBC in projecting a distinctive Britishness? How should the BBC respond to the Johnson Government's hostility? Is that hostility merited? Should the BBC be broken up?

This book covers the full spectrum of views on the corporation. Within these pages there are the perspectives of BBC lifers, BBC bashers and BBC true believers. Leading television executives, media academics, prominent journalists of varying stripes, economists and politicians all have their say. There are points of agreement, but there are profound points of disagreement. If the BBC is an important aspect of national life in Britain, then this book is, to some extent, a debate about the nature of national life in Britain today – the nature of democracy and its safeguards, the nature of culture, and the nature of digital technology's impact on our daily lives.

The BBC's founding principles almost a century ago were for it to inform, educate and entertain. Few support the idea of an unreconstructed BBC standing in magisterial Reithian immutability amid the torrent of streamed, subscription-based rival content. Even the BBC's most ardent supporters in this book acknowledge myriad imperfections. John Simpson, to give one prominent example, admits to being occasionally "enraged" by the corporation he has served since 1966. For Simpson, the BBC is actually a fragile organisation, but one whose continued existence matters for audiences across the globe. He expects a future BBC to be slimmed-down and to focus on "core activities" while leaving most entertainment content to Netflix and other channels.

The BBC's continued existence has been brought into question by the rumblings issuing from No. 10 Downing Street and Boris Johnson's chief adviser, Dominic Cummings. There have been frequent disputes between the BBC and politicians of all parties but Raymond Snoddy contends that the "depth and range of current animosity appears unprecedented". Rob Wilson is one of the most outspoken critics of the BBC in these pages, and he spells out why he believes the corporation's days could be numbered. For him the BBC is "a 20th century construct trying to survive in the fast-paced digital world of the 21st century". The whole thing – its governance, management, decision-making structure and culture – is no longer fit for purpose. Saddled by moribund structures, the next decade could be its last.

The licence fee naturally constitutes the main mustering point for debate in this book. Is it an outdated and illegitimate poll tax that restricts consumer choice (an "archaic funding mechanism", as David Cox puts it), or a means of funding a public good that fulfils an important social role? This connects with the wider question of whether broadcasting should be purely determined by the market. Andrew Graham argues that it shouldn't. The licence fee, he contends, is not a fee to watch any particular programme but to "maintain the system as a whole and so increase the benefit for us all". He adds: "The BBC has the potential to 'reach the parts that others do not' and by ensuring the quality of UK broadcasting across the board far from diminishing choice it adds to it. A subscription model, necessarily restricted to those who can pay and providing programming only for what viewers already know they like, is a diminishing experience for them and for us all."

The licence fee has other defenders. While contending that the BBC is staffed "near exclusively by gushing liberals and centrist Blairite refugees", Damian Reilly offers full-throated support for the fee. The BBC "genuinely is the envy of the world", with its "blessed freedom from chasing ratings" acting as a brake on the race to the cultural bottom. Reilly might fall short of urging a manning of the barricades, but he is not far off. "People take to the streets to protest at the idea of our other great national miracle of civilisation, the NHS, being opened to even the smallest fraction to market forces," he writes. "Why not then the same fear of upward pressure naturally being exerted on the cost of a BBC subscription?" Peter Snow, in his Foreword above, is fierce in his defence of Auntie, too. To undermine a broadcasting system that provides advertisement-free programming with universal appeal would constitute, as he sees it, "an act of mindless self-harm". The BBC is an arm of the people and not of government, and Snow believes that needs to be cherished.

Like Reilly, Gillian Reynolds views the BBC as an important guardian of British cultural life, which has fostered nationally and internationally important writers such as Tom Stoppard and Lee Hall. The corporation also plays a key role in sustaining the nation's musical life. She takes the example of The Proms. Even when selling 90 per cent of tickets, The Proms will show a balance sheet loss. "The licence fee covers that loss," says Reynolds, "a debt worth paying if it underscores the survival of music in schools and concert halls all over the UK." Jean Seaton also sees the corporation's significance as transcending a particular moment, programme or piece of output. "The BBC is the always-reformable institution that makes the public space of our national imaginations bigger and more generous," she argues.

Others believe that the broadcasting landscape is shifting in more dramatic ways. BBC executives should accept that change is coming, argues Owen Bennett-Jones, and plan for significant alterations to the "unsustainable" licence fee. But he fears reaction rather than pro-activity from the corporation. "In all likelihood, however, the BBC will cling on to the licence fee for as long as possible until an alternative is forced upon it," he writes. "And that is where the real peril lies."

Andrew Graham, as well as arguing in favour of the licence fee, contends that the growth of echo chambers and the rapid distribution of fake news has made the role of the BBC as a universally available "truth-teller" more important than ever. Why, he says, kill a trusted deliverer of news when such content is becoming scarcer? Will Wyatt takes a similar stance. The corporation is the UK's "strongest seeker after truth", he claims, and any organisation which "can interview its chief executive to destruction on air has a rare cultural integrity". The BBC needs to propose its own way forward and believe in itself, forging its own reconstituted Reithian vision for a future of streamed and personalised content.

Remaining a step ahead of the Government that will ultimately define its future – and accepting that change needs to be far-reaching – is a point also emphasised by Peter Bennett-Jones. "By recognising that reform has to be radical in a changing market, and by arguing the case for the retention of key elements of what is a unique national asset, the BBC is more likely to prevent the barbarians knocking down their gates and destroying its very essence."

While not explicitly referring to any barbarian hordes, Simon Albury offers a detailed analysis of how he believes the Johnson Government, with Cummings tweaking the strings, has undermined the Press, Ofcom and the Commons Digital, Culture, Sport and Media Committee, thereby polluting the forums for debating the BBC's future. "The Government hostility to the BBC and to democratic processes sets the wrong environment for a reasonable debate about the licence fee," writes Albury. Taking up a similar theme, Steven Barnett claims that the BBC faces its most savage political environment since the election of Margaret Thatcher in 1979, and that now – as then – it needs a powerful friend in high places.

Brian Winston and Matthew Winston offer a historical perspective on the evolution of the BBC's funding and its parameters, and make a plea for lessons to be learnt from the original Royal Charter. They also question the coherence of the concept of due impartiality. In a similar vein, Ivor Gaber considers the vexed question of BBC bias, and argues that the picture is more nuanced than commonly recognised.

Fiona Chesterton pens a letter to what she imagines to be the first female director-general and makes a plea for the new incumbent to make some significant reforms. Elsewhere, Jane Martinson argues that the Johnson Government's thirst for controlling communication has made the role of director-general a poisoned chalice. The need to protect the corporation is, she says, urgent. Finally John Mair embarks on an odyssey into the blogosphere of the future, imagining just what Dominic Cummings might be posting in 2027.

Turning the lens onto sport, I argue that the corporation's pursuit of a younger audience is causing something of an identity crisis, as it simultaneously targets the young demographic while feeling pangs of responsibility to its loyal, older audience. Similarly, Iain Dale argues that, instead of innovating, the corporation is issuing mixed messages to its different target demographics. "There seems to be more interest in an obsession with attracting young listeners and viewers despite an utter failure to cater for their needs in non-linear broadcasting," he writes. "And this obsession leads to a total failure to cater for the overwhelmingly majority of their core, older listeners." The issue of the youth audience concerns other contributors, with Richard Sambrook arguing that a perceived lack of relevance to the under-30 audience is sharpening the existential danger to the corporation.

Post-Brexit, a number of contributors argue that the BBC now carries greater significance due to its ability to enable Britain to project a form of 'soft power' on the world stage. However, it is arguably now power of a different sort – the harder power that comes in the early days of government following a clear electoral majority – that media-watchers and the British public at large should he focusing on. As the chapters in this book make clear, the tensions between the corporation and the Government are real, and how those tensions are settled will have a major bearing on not just broadcasting in Britain but on public life in a new decade.

Tom Bradshaw, Cheltenham, February 2020

Chapter 1

Just Imagine: the BBC is a broadcasting wonder and not to be discarded lightly

**The BBC faces formidable difficulties. It must propose
how its values and purposes can be carried into a
future of individuality and choice. Funding will
have to change. The BBC is too important
to the UK at home and overseas to be wilfully damaged.
Will Wyatt knows it well from the inside – he
was a BBC Brahmin**

The nation is split. The fault lines are many following a referendum, a general election and thirty years of blinkered policy making. Political discourse is brutish and divisive, egged on by solipsistic commentary and the crude tribal gatherings of social media. Our leaders are desperate to bring people together, for the United Kingdom appears to be fracturing just as it slips anchor from Europe to sail as a brave lone voyager.

If we had an organisation that carried our flag throughout the world...

As the UK announces itself anew across the globe wouldn't it be marvellous if there were a British organisation which carried our flag proudly throughout the world as the most trusted supplier of news, the most sought-after account of world events for those in repressive regimes? Wouldn't it help us if that organisation, albeit far from perfect, was also deemed the most reliable in its reporting on air and online in the United Kingdom?

And wouldn't it be splendid if it also covered live on television the great bonding occasions that reflect the heart and history of the nation, D-Day Anniversary celebrations, the Annual Service of Remembrance, Trooping the Colour and the like?

Imagine, also, that the same organisation had created many of our cultural reference points from *Dad's Army* and *Monty Python* to *Doctor Who* and the television *Pride and Prejudice*, *Absolutely Fabulous* and *Fleabag*; that it continued to make or commission some of the best television drama, develop some of the best comic talents on both television and radio, was a byword for the inventiveness and range of natural history programmes; and transmitted headline-making investigations into national and international scandals and injustices.

What if the same outfit regularly offered history and science programmes authored by leading academics, while on radio and in podcasts it gave a platform to the leading thinkers, artists and writers as part of a year-round service of talks, discussions, interviews and debates?

We're dreaming now, but could it be that this body was also the chief provider of programmes made specifically for British children, and, say, also ran symphony orchestras in London, Manchester, Scotland and Wales that played to audiences around the country and live on air? And mounted and broadcast the world's biggest classical music festival? And reported on life in the United Kingdom through local and regional news, funding a partnership with local media to support local democracy? And could create hugely popular entertainment shows? And music services for young adults seeded with information and advice campaigns?

We do have one

Enough, you cry. You've heard it all before. That doesn't make it less true. Make no mistake, these, and more, are national assets, invaluable to a nation anxious about its very nation-ness. If the BBC is in peril, they are in peril.

The sense of impending crisis has been churning below ground and now bursts into view. Tony Hall is to stand down as director-general and a change in leadership is a moment of vulnerability. A new regime in government lets it be known via grunts and grumbles that it has a 'something must be done' view of the BBC. Political threats are not new but it's best to assume they are real and this one comes with an ideological edge just as seismic forces are reshaping the broadcasting and communication landscape.

Boris Johnson's in-house guru, Dominic Cummings, ran a think tank which in 2004 claimed "the BBC is a determined propagandist with a coherent ideology". The Right should seek to undermine its credibility with "a well-funded campaign that involves bringing out whistleblowers armed with internal memos and taped conversations of meetings".

In 34 years in the BBC I don't recall any document or meeting the transcription of which would fuel his engine of suspicion. The fact is that for a committed politician or propagandist anything that is not overtly for you must be against you.

As the centre ground collapses, it is ever harder to be or seen to be impartial, a core purpose of the BBC. The prisms through which its coverage is viewed bend their rays ever more sharply. Even so, the Ofcom special review of BBC News and Current Affairs in 2019 stated: "The BBC remains the UK's primary source for news. Despite an uncertain political environment, it has maintained its reputation among most people for trusted and accurate reporting. Audiences told us that these were a news provider's most important attributes, particularly during breaking news stories. In a world of fake news and disinformation online, they said they turn to the BBC for a reliable take on events."

The BBC must always be questioned and tested on its performance but with the internet spewing a deafening babble of lies, propaganda and mischief we need such a bulwark of reliability more than ever. However irritated and sceptical a government, what do our people gain, and how is democracy served, by inflicting damage on this public good?

Where was binge viewing a decade ago?

Political winds may well blow this way and that. The deeper difficulty for the BBC is that the current chill gusts across a hopeful battleground for its critics: the speed of technological and consumer change. The tectonic plates of communication have shifted. What media means and how it is received is in question.

Streaming services invest eye-watering sums in new drama series and films (Netflix's budget was $15bn last year, and it has 167 million global subscribers). This is transforming entertainment in the home. Where was 'binge viewing' ten years ago?

The young are difficult to reach for the BBC

Many of the young have never known a world without the internet, which for them is the chief mode of viewing. The BBC finds it hard to reach them. The world is at their touch via the phones in their pockets and by their pillows. YouTube is the leading form of visual entertainment for children. The internet is not a wonder to them, it just is. As was the radio when I was a boy, no thought of what came before even if as exciting as a magic lantern show.

Learn from Dad's Army

The BBC faces formidable difficulties. Even so it should heed Corporal Jones: "Don't panic." The BBC has long been an innovator in technology and programmes. It now has to innovate its own future, not merely for institutional survival but to ensure that its purposes and values – impartial news, guaranteeing that the full breadth of broadcasting is available to all, representing the nation to itself in its ceremonies and history, documenting its life, telling its stories in drama and comedy through British creative talent – are carried into the future.

I hope that the BBC has had some clever people working on this. It is essential that it proposes its own way forward. By getting on the front foot it will best be able to devise a plan which allows those purposes to thrive. Meet the challenge. Make the case. Others will punt proposals aplenty caring nothing for the ideals of what we used to call broadcasting. It is for the BBC to spell out the unique value of its services and how they can be reconfigured: a Reithian vision for the streaming, personalised future.

Death by a thousand cuts

It has been the licence fee that enabled, in fact demanded, those purposes in the past. It is guaranteed till 2027 but by then it is hard to see it renewed in its present form. Already the BBC is carrying the cost of many licences for the over 75s. Soon failure to have a licence will probably not be a criminal offence. Psychologically that cuts the knot and a mass defection is possible. Will the BBC have the resources to chase the non-payers and fund the lawyers to take them to civil courts? Many favour making the licence voluntary believing that while many would no longer pay, others would pay more. This would be an enormous risk more likely to bring a crippling cut in income and a drastic reduction in services.

Advertising on the BBC is not feasible. It would probably bust Channel 4 and Channel 5, would slice pieces off ITV, and probably destroy commercial radio. Not a sensible route for any government or consumers.

Pay per view? It would be a service, but no longer the BBC

Subscription is a popular alternative and now at last the technology will make it possible for most households. But not all and there lies a problem. The BBC could survive and possibly even thrive as a subscription service but its imperative would immediately become the retention and growth of subscriptions. That would lead to money being piled into premium drama and comedy, and anything which doesn't drive those subs being thrown overboard.

Radio would have to be cross-subsidised or rely on public donations, unless you want ads on Radio 4. Good luck with that *PM*.

Articulate the common land of broadcasting

I think that the long-term solution will be a combination of funding: a licence fee as long as it be retained, a subscription element, voluntary funds, commercial partnerships where safe and compatible with core BBC values. I believe there will be a large constituency of citizens who see the BBC as an integral part of what makes this country what it is and see its programmes as a signifier of British culture. If the average age of BBC One viewers is 61 then a lot must be in their forties and around for a while yet. I also doubt that any government will truly wish to damage beyond repair Britain's only world media brand and a crucial element for Britain's second great world class sector, the creative industries.

The BBC must make the case for what, in the world of individuality, choice and selection, we all should have available to us: the national stories and glories, the common land of broadcasting. It must build an army of supporters and a high-profile cadre of shock troops.

It must **believe** in itself.

The UK must retain its strongest seeker after truth. The BBC has its failings, for an organisation is its people and people make mistakes. But an organisation which can interview its chief executive to destruction on air has a rare cultural integrity. It is not an outfit to be discarded lightly.

About the contributor

Will Wyatt CBE was a journalist, producer and head of documentary features at the BBC before becoming managing director of BBC Television (1991-96) and chief executive BBC Broadcast (1996- 99). He is the author of *The Fun Factory - A Life in the BBC* and two other books. He is a past president of the Royal Television Society, was chair of the University of the Arts London, Human Capital Ltd. and Racecourse Media Group. He was a director of Eurobet and Vitec plc.

Chapter 2

Adequate reform of the BBC requires a Herculean effort

The BBC needs to slim down the range of its output and rethink what it means to be a public service broadcaster in the 21st century, argues LBC radio presenter Iain Dale

Throughout the history of the BBC, governments of all shades have indulged in messy spats with the corporation. The current 'war' between Boris Johnson's government and the BBC is little different to all the others. However, the BBC's fight is not just with the government of the day, it is with its competition. The battle for eyeballs and ears has never been more cutthroat, and if the BBC fails to acknowledge that it has no divine right to continue to exist in its current form it will inevitably sink into decades of decline and stasis.

How relevant is Reith?

The key thing the BBC needs to do now is to rethink what its purpose is. Is its remit still to "inform, educate and entertain" or does it need to move away from its Reithian heritage? From there it needs to get on the front foot on how it is funded. Instead of leaving it to government to dictate the terms of its financing it should immediately start to think about alternative forms of financing rather than just repeat is mantra that the licence fee is the best form of funding there is. Once upon a time that may well have been the case. In the media environment of the 2020s, it isn't.

Viewers are used to subscribing to Sky, to Netflix, to Amazon Prime, to Disney and now to BritBox. All these media providers have to provide an offering that leads to their customers wanting to part with their money. The BBC does not. We have to pay £157.50 whether we like it or not. Let's not beat about the bush. It's a poll tax. And if you don't pay it you can face a prison sentence. One in ten court cases in this country revolve around the non-payment of TV licences.

What is public service broadcasting in 2020? Surely it has to revolve around providing broadcast services that the commercial sector won't, or can't. That's not to say that it shouldn't provide entertainment programmes too, but one thing it should not be doing is competing on every level with commercial broadcasters.

In early February BBC News and Current Affairs announced a further round of cuts to their TV and radio offerings, involving 450 job losses – very few of them among BBC management, obviously. Just a few days later the BBC triumphantly announced the creation of 20 new online radio shows and podcasts, most of which seemed to be specifically designed to compete with existing offerings from commercial radio. The contrast between the two announcements could not be clearer. It's as if one part of the BBC doesn't talk to another, and the senior management can't see the wood for the trees.

Market distortion by stealth

The BBC is a monopoly broadcaster and often tries, by stealth, to knock the competition out of the arena. That's what the announcement about the new podcasts and programmes is all about. They're doing it in the world of podcasting too, despite being very late to the podcast party. They can do it because they have the marketing ability to trounce any competitors. They did it to Oneword Radio, a digital station devoted to the world of books and the arts, which launched in 2000. The BBC decided it couldn't possibly tolerate that, so created BBC7 (eventually to become Radio 4 Extra) and eventually Oneword was driven out of business. They did it in the magazine world by creating all sorts of BBC branded magazines, which drove several competitors to the wall. And now they're trying to do it in the world of music radio and podcasts.

Each year the BBC spends around £2.4bn on its TV offerings, but a comparatively paltry £650m on radio. BBC 1 eats up half the TV budget, while a mere £68m is spent on the BBC News channel, and only £10m on BBC Parliament. In all, only around half of the BBC's expenditure of more than £5bn is spent on programming. This proportion needs to rise. As does the proportion spent on news and current affairs.

The BBC is our gateway to the world. It has a worldwide reputation which is second to none. The BBC World Service – which is largely funded by government grant – should be nurtured, cherished and expanded. It's all part of Britain's soft power. If only we could say the same for its TV equivalent, BBC World. It ought to be a competitor to CNN, Al Jazeera English and the new NBC/Sky Channel which will launch later this year, but it isn't. Given its meagre budget, it's not surprising. Serious consideration should be given to combining it with the BBC News channel.

Political cuts

At a time when interest in politics is at an all-time high, what does the BBC do? It axes its most popular political TV show, *This Week*. It follows up this mad decision by cancelling the award-winning *Victoria Derbyshire* show, without even having the politeness to inform its host. She read about it in *The Times*. It treats its lead and best political interviewer, Andrew Neil, with utter disdain and allows *Question Time* to become a bear-pit of a programme which many politicians now, understandably, refuse to appear on. It continually cuts the budget of its flagship daily current affairs show, *Newsnight*, to the extent where ground-breaking reporting and award-winning investigative films are relegated in importance and cheap-to-book panels take their place.

In this new 20th century media environment the BBC must recognise it can't do everything, nor should it. Other national broadcasters don't. Look at ARD in Germany, or NHK in Japan. NHK has four linear TV stations plus two satellite stations, and only three radio stations. As Philip Patrick wrote in *The Spectator*, "NHK's presentation is low key and modest. Unlike the BBC's shouty, self-promotion with the endlessly repeated trailers that make you feel like you are being grabbed by the lapels and screamed at, NHK's presenters are mild-mannered and respectful and not noticeably chosen for their youth or attractiveness. They appear rather humbled by the privilege of serving the public through the national broadcaster." Contrast this with the BBC, whose incessant trailers for its programmes are again designed to smash the competition into the ground. Given the time it devotes to advertising its own programmes, it might as well be allowed to take commercial advertising. NHK doesn't fight wars on all fronts. It concentrates, in an understated way, on some key core areas and leaves the rest to other broadcasters.

Open goals for savings

Both Radio 1 and Radio 2 could be privatised and funded by advertising. That's more than £100 million off the running costs of the BBC at a stroke, not to mention the one-off revenue a sale of those two stations would attract.

The BBC has spent £211.5 million for a three-year contract to show recorded football highlights on *Match of the Day* and its sister programmes. Is this really value for money given the fact that only 4 million people watch *Match of the Day*, and the vast majority of those probably have a Sky Sports subscription anyway? The corporation should no longer bid for major sporting events and instead reinvest the money in covering less popular sports which the commercial channels don't or can't cover. The BBC's investment in women's football, for example, has done more to popularise the sport than anything else.

The identity crisis of BBC local radio

BBC local radio has been a basket case for many years, despite being funded to the tune of more than £160 million a year. It doesn't know what it's for. One year it's told to be more like LBC and do more local phone-ins. The next year it introduces a new imaging package where the strapline for each of the 39 stations is the same: "The Sound of [area] and all the music you love". So are they speech or music stations? Which is it? Most of them have programme schedules which are unfocussed and too diverse in content. The local seems to have been ripped out of BBC local radio. Again, they are trying too hard to compete with their commercial rivals.

I want the BBC to succeed. I want it to thrive. I am a huge admirer of much of what it does. But it is a wallowing, bureaucratic institution, held back by an institutionalised management more interested in covering their own backs than promoting innovation and giving viewers and listeners what they want. There seems to be more interest in an obsession with attracting young listeners and viewers despite an utter failure to cater for their needs in non-linear broadcasting. And this obsession leads to a total failure to cater for the overwhelmingly majority of their core, older listeners.

The Herculean labour of BBC reform

All this demonstrates that whoever succeeds Lord Hall as director-general and Sir David Clementi as chairman of the BBC have the most herculean of tasks on their hands.

What is needed is a duo who can think radically, aren't afraid to confront vested interests and are seen as transformational individuals, with a track record of reform and innovation. The last thing the BBC needs is two BBC lifers in charge.

About the contributor

Iain Dale presents the Evening Show on LBC Radio and is a contributor to various BBC news and political programmes.

Chapter 3

BBC managers must stay one step ahead of the barbarians at the corporation's gates

Peter Bennett-Jones has unique takes on the BBC as viewer, supplier, uber-agent and a mastermind behind Comic Relief and Sport Relief. He argues that BBC executives will need fallback options when it comes to negotiating the future of the corporation's funding

I have three perspectives on our national broadcaster as it approaches its centenary in 2022 with political opponents and rival media interests knocking on its hallowed Portland Place portals.

The first is as a supplier since the 1980s – of talented artists, writers, actors, directors, journalists and presenters through my agency PBJ Management and sister agency KBJ Management. I have also overseen the supply of scores of multi-genre television and radio titles through founding and chairing Tiger Aspect Productions and, more recently, Burning Bright Productions. Those titles include *Billy Elliot, Charlie and Lola, Robin Hood,* and *The Vicar of Dibley.*

My second vantage point is as a partner. In my role as a founding trustee and long-term chair of Comic Relief and its sibling Sport Relief I have helped to negotiate and build a partnership over 25 years to establish and grow what has become one of the UK's best-known and most-loved charities.

My third point of view is, like all licence fee-payers, as a punter – a viewer and a listener.

Why the BBC?

At the outset I should make it crystal clear that I consider the BBC to be a unique force for good and an institution for which it is worth fighting vigorously and vocally. It has been the nation's glue for decades – universally entertaining, educating and informing generations in a consistent application of the Reithian principles in a commercial and advertising-free zone.

The BBC's cultural impact and importance is vital to the country's well-being, whether it be through providing opportunity for the creative community by means of training, commissioning and nurturing talent; through promoting classical music with the magnificent Proms and the BBC orchestras; through reaching out globally via the World Service; educating the next generation through its children's television services; through its news services, radio and online initiatives, and through its broadly excellent national and regional output on screen, online and on radio.

I have witnessed at close hand the corporation firing on all cylinders on *Red Nose Day* campaigns and a mighty, multi-faceted machine and force for good it can be. The BBC has no equal, anywhere, and the licence fee represents exceedingly good value for money.

Why is the BBC in peril?

And yet this multi-billion-pound public service broadcasting beast is more vulnerable to hostile outside and internal forces than it ever has been. There is global and local competition in the digital age with markets fragmenting, combined with a political opposition from the most hostile and philistine government for decades. Prime Minister Johnson has already fired an opening salvo having had his tail tweaked by the corporation during the recent election campaign and appears to be limbering up for a fight.

Immediate issues around decriminalisation of licence fee payment evasion, the over-75 funding arrangements, audience fragmentation, reach and ratings are all having to be grappled with. Tony Hall, the outgoing director-general, has already been seen off as the headwinds gather force and who can blame him for moving on? The dual role of acting as chief executive and editor-in-chief is no longer sustainable and the responsibilities should be separated into executive and editorial roles.

Why the licence fee?

The very concept of the licence fee funding model is under threat and the odds are against its survival in its current form after 2027 at the end of the current Royal Charter. The BBC and its new leadership will need to be ahead of the curve with fresh thinking to manage these challenges and to avoid having terms dictated to them. Crucially, even if their first position is retention of the universal fee they will need fallback options.

The BBC is in some respects schizophrenic, being caught between the need to both entertain and to inform its audiences. One of the central problems is the tension between the need to change the output with the requirement to offer universal service provision. All the while the managers have to be aware of Ofcom's eagle-eyed micro-managers monitoring assorted quotas and obligations, preventing in the process the broadcaster implementing reforms and cuts to services.

The result is that the BBC is now too big and is obliged to do too much. It needs to do less and to make the case for this. It should be possible to run a credible public service broadcaster on an income of less than the current £3.8bn. Work needs to take place on lower guaranteed income models. What, for example, could be done with £2.5bn?

Is the BBC innocent?

In some respects the corporation has only itself to blame. It can be institutionally arrogant, over-bureaucratic, is too often a nasty employer, lacks trained executive as opposed to editorial leaders and has in some cases been too compliant when needing to face down government and too aggressive when asserting its perceived divine right to aggressively hold all and sundry to direct account.

I have twice been on the receiving end of BBC News scalp-hunting exercises in my charity chairing capacity, with Comic Relief and Save the Children. I did not consider it to be a fair contest in either instance and the story coverage appeared to be campaigning dressed up as reporting. I feel that it makes a mockery of the oft-made claim to be impartial in approach. Unconscious bias and headline-creating within this powerful institution is endemic and needs to be recognised.

My medicine to save the corporation

It is time for radical thinking to future-proof the BBC and its values.cIt is the moment to start fundamental reform. The BBC should be sub-divided, with news and entertainment functions subject to different funding, expert commissioning, and fresh editorial and governance arrangements. It has always struck me as illogical that the same editorial policies and principles are applied to news output as to comedy and drama. Impartiality as a north star to follow is essential for news gathering and broadcasting, however tough to deliver, whereas partiality is almost an essential element of satirical comedy, which is now a threatened species.

My experience as both a supplier and partner over recent years is that the BBC is so cowed in the wake of perceived editorial and management failings over matters such as the Iraq War coverage, Blue Peter 'cheating' and the Jimmy Savile fiasco that it now applies a safety first policy and bureaucratic process to all output, making it increasingly anodyne and risk-averse, with the side-effect of no longer being the broadcaster of choice for independent programme suppliers and their projects. Suppliers are prepared to accept that the BBC cannot always be competitive with budgets but become exasperated by the sclerotic commissioning and editorial processes.

Market failure in commissioning

As in any market where supply heavily outstrips demand, the buyer is able to get away with shoddy procurement processes – this is rampant at the BBC and it and its staff, suppliers and consumers would benefit from a return to a more enlightened and confident approach. This could be achieved by offering its excellent entertainment output, from glorious global hit *Strictly Come Dancing* to *Fleabag*, on a subscription and digital delivery payment basis, while ring-fencing and publicly funding output of importance which needs subsidy because of market failure and intrinsic merit. Urgent thought needs to be applied to how pay platforms can be put into place alongside Freeview.

Candidates for protection would be *CBBC* and *Cbeebies*, which are beacons of BBC editorial and management excellence and in need of meaningful financial support as they continue to attract and retain young viewers, the current holy grail. Many aspects of BBC Network Radio also represent outstanding value for money and offer superb quality which needs cherishing and protecting.

Subscription-based funding would also prevent the significant problem of prosecutions for fee payment evasion. Last year there were close to 130,000 prosecutions, with over 1,000 going to court. The current system not only clogs up the criminal justice system but also penalises the poorer elements of society, many of whom have a minimal interest in BBC output. There has to be a better way. Come what may, the BBC has to budget for the mitigate the effects of decriminalisation as it looks to be politically inevitable despite the 2015 review findings.

News for news

Where would this leave BBC News, a cornerstone of public service provision? This is the function of the BBC that is most in need of internal reform and there are encouraging recent signs that this is at last being realised and addressed. Deeper reform is needed. Currently set up with a series of largely ungovernable and duplicative competing fiefdoms, it appears often to be highly inefficient, expensive and accident-prone.

The excellence of much of BBC News' purpose and reporting could be protected, maintained and indeed improved under a new structure, more akin to ITN with its News, Broadcast and Production divisions supplying a range of broadcasters.

BBC News (incorporating current affairs) should be accountable to a distinct board, with a debate to be had as to how best to fund it – whether it be subscription, advertising or a ring-fenced central funding deal from tax revenues similar to the way in which all the World Service output was financed via the Foreign & Commonwealth Office until recently. Critical national services from healthcare to education are centrally funded, and could there be a version which worked for the BBC, retaining the element of independence from government it currently enjoys?

Keeping the BBC independent?

Although this independence from government control is in many ways an illusion, some form of meaningful separation and accountability is a prerequisite under any new funding formula and various options need modelling.

The BBC will have much to celebrate in its 2022 centenary year. It needs not only to remind its viewers and listeners of the glories it has supplied in the past and continues to produce but also to demonstrate that it is capable of adapting to a changing world and will be in position to remain a vital and unique national asset. Vitally, it needs to retain broad public support, which will be the main weapon to wield when under attack.

This calls for a separation of functions, a reduction in size and scope, being allowed off the commercial leash, especially in respect of the exploitation of its precious archive, and an ongoing commitment to excellence in all it does – attracting the nation's best talent and thereby entertaining, educating, informing and at times uniting its audiences.

Keep ahead, not behind, the curve

Survival is more likely to be achieved satisfactorily by the BBC management remaining a step ahead of the government which ultimately controls its future. By recognising that reform has to be radical in a changing market, and by arguing the case for the retention of key elements of what is a unique national asset, the BBC is more likely to prevent the barbarians knocking down their gates and destroying its very essence.

About the contributor

Peter Bennett-Jones is an agent and producer. He founded PBJ Management and the Tiger Television in 1987, stepping down in 2011. Long-term clients include Rowan Atkinson, Lenny Henry, Armando Iannucci, Sally Phillips, Tim Minchin, Nina Conti, Reeves & Mortimer and *The League of Gentlemen*. Tiger Aspect produced over 500 comedy, drama, factual and animation titles for domestic and international broadcasters and distributors during his tenure. He was a founding trustee of Comic Relief and chaired the charity from 1998-2013, and Save the Children UK from 2015-2019. He was a board member of the National Theatre and has also served on the boards of RADA, the Oxford Playhouse, the Millennium Promise and Liverpool Everyman-Playhouse.

Chapter 4

Protect the BBC's purposes, not the obsolete institution

It's the New Broadcasting House top brass who are imperilling our national broadcaster. They should be dispossessed, says former ITV executive David Cox

The roots of the BBC's current difficulties lie in its archaic funding mechanism. Now that its monopoly of both output and audience is long dead, fewer than half of those aged 16 to 24 see any BBC programmes in an average week. Yet, everyone who watches any broadcast television must be covered by a licence, so people who watch and listen only to commercial output are still required to pay for the BBC's.

Penalise the licence non-payers?

Each year, there are more than 100,000 prosecutions for evasion: more women are prosecuted for this offence than for any other. Campaigners complain about unfairness and "the criminalisation of poverty". The government has promised to address this issue irrespective of any deeper rethink. If criminal prosecution is jettisoned, the BBC believes it will be stripped of £200 million a year, while losing the contributions of indigent over-75-year-olds and compensating female staff claiming discrimination.

Bigger sharks in the broadcast sea than the BBC

Far more serious perils threaten licence fee revenue. On-demand streaming giants are luring people away from broadcast television. The young watch only half as much conventional TV as they did a decade ago (Ofcom annual report, 2017). People who stick to streamed programming are not required to buy a licence, so long as they stay off the BBC's iPlayer, and fewer householders are therefore likely to bother paying the licence fee. What's more, people who do watch live TV, but only on phones or tablets, can easily avoid payment.

Nevertheless, the corporation's current management insist on clinging to the existing system. This unbending stance has led them into efforts to preserve the status quo that have compounded the BBC's troubles.

Is the BBC still the 'national voice'?

To defend its claim to a near-universal charge, the BBC Brahmins have fought to maintain its status as the "national voice" as new media have emerged. This has meant expanding beyond conventional broadcasting into fresh fields, like multichannel TV, the internet and podcasting, however well these are already supplied. This has diverted cash from programmes and sparked complaints of unfair market distortion.

Another aim of the corporation has been to heighten the BBC's popularity, in the hope of scaring off meddlesome politicians. To maximise audiences, entertainment has been prioritised over other functions. Yet in this field the BBC's new rivals are far outgunning it. Today, Netflix alone spends £12 billion a year on new programming for its 160 million subscribers (Netflix fourth quarter earnings report, 2018). From its own endangered income stream, the BBC manages to spend just £3 billion a year on all of its TV and radio output. Deep-pocketed newcomers aren't just grabbing its viewers and listeners: they're driving up the cost of rights, studios and performers.

As a public sector organisation, the BBC cannot call on lenders and investors to boost its firepower. Nor does its funding mechanism allow it to extract from its devotees the maximum they might be willing to pay. So, its audience share seems bound to fade, with its income, its popularity, and public support for the licence fee following suit. Already, 74 per cent of the public want the fee axed, according to a poll conducted by Public First in December.

Time for the BBC to go back to basics?

Yet even if the BBC could hold on to both its popularity and its overall share of our attention, delivering entertainment wouldn't be enough to legitimise what amounts to a poll tax. The corporation must also provide services which are essential to society but won't be offered in the market-place. Unfortunately, its concentration on popularity and scale has undermined its delivery of information and education.

Inevitably, their resources have had to be cut. Programmes like *Newsnight* have had their modest budgets slashed and reporters axed so that DJs and sports presenters can be paid a million pound-plus salaries. Worse, demanding programmes have been starved of attention and commitment.

Has the BBC lost its 'ringmaster' role?

In the face of the major crises that have recently beset the country— climate change, the EU referendum and the Brexit election—the BBC stands charged with falling down on its most important job. It's accused of neglecting to examine properly what was at issue, preferring to provide platforms for contending protagonists, satisfied that so long as rival pronouncements were balanced, they didn't need to be interrogated.

At the same time, allegations of bias, from both ends of the political spectrum, have grown louder, and not without cause. Since, at intervals, the BBC must renegotiate the licence fee with the government, it has to be wary of the politically powerful, not just of those in office but of those who one day may be. It must also respect the orthodoxy of the prevailing cultural elite. Therefore, those who challenge established ideas and institutions have always tended to distrust the corporation. Meanwhile, the conservative-minded believe establishment organisations like the BBC are in thrall to 'progressive' thinking. In December, YouGov reported that only 44 per cent of us trust the BBC to be impartial.

Is the end nigh for the BBC?

So, must it be left to atrophy? Or might the interlinked problems engendered by the obsolete model on which it operates somehow be resolved? Boris Johnson said during the election campaign that he is "looking at" changing the basis on which the BBC functions. What could he do?

When the Conservatives were still in opposition, they summoned a posse of independent experts to ponder the BBC's future. This became the Broadcasting Policy Group; I was a member. Our recommendations went down well with the Tory top brass, but were deemed too unnerving for a party seeking power. Today, they've become even more pertinent, and a Commons majority of 80 leaves no excuse for funk.

Our manifesto for the future of the BBC

We concluded that the BBC's outworn set-up would have to be dismantled; yet both its entertainment and public service functions must be enabled to thrive thereafter. Our key finding was that, to prevent them from conflicting, they would have to be separated. We proposed that the BBC's most successful asset, its entertainment power-house, should be liberated from its current constraints and equipped to fight its corner in the market-place. Public service functions would still be publicly funded, but in return their quality and impartiality would have to be secured. These principles could still provide the basis for a workable arrangement.

BBC Entertainment Corp?

BBC entertainment, drama, reality TV and so forth could be run by a public corporation administered like Channel 4 but focused solely on popular output for Britain and the world. Its TV services could be funded by global subscribers, as Netflix is, though it might feature a variable tariff, so heavy users would pay more while others could pay less than the current licence-fee. Its pop radio services could be funded through advertising, like all such existing services apart from the BBC's.

Its British focus would give it an edge in the UK, but competition from overseas rivals would keep it on its mettle. Competition might also provide the key to improving Britain's public service fare. Before the 1990 Broadcasting Act, ITV franchises were awarded partly according to the worthiness of the applicants' programme plans. The resulting contests spawned the likes of *World in Action*, *The World at War*, *The South Bank Show*, *Weekend World* and *Walden* (disclosure: I worked on the last two), which were often considered to outshine their BBC counterparts. In response, the corporation upped its game.

A Public Broadcasting Authority?

To create a similar spur to excellence, public service programming could be put out to competitive tender, instead of being entrusted to one organisation. An arm's-length body like Ofcom could determine what was required, and then disburse funds, as the British Film Institute does to film-makers, on a contestable basis. It could commission from all-comers, including new entities hived off from the BBC's factual departments, and distribute output not just through TV and radio but also through print and the internet.

Such an arrangement ought not only to promote quality; it could also better fend off suspicions of bias. The slim-line commissioning body should be more resistant to establishment pressure. Contributors drawn from a variety of sources would be less susceptible to collective groupthink. A scheme like this would cost far less than the licence-fee brings in, most of which is hogged by entertainment. The modest sum required might be raised from a bolt-on to council tax, proportionally levied so the poor need no longer pay as much as the rich.

Re-engineer the BBC now

Rejigging the BBC's functions along these lines couldn't be done overnight. Technical obstacles, deliberately created in part by the corporation's management to obstruct change, would have to be overcome.

However, there is time to do this: the BBC's existing Royal Charter doesn't expire until 2027. All the same, to meet even that target, decisions would best be made soon.

A first step could be taken in 2022, when the licence-fee will be reviewed. Its level could be reduced, and, to compensate, the iPlayer could start charging for premiere airings of premium programmes. This wouldn't be beyond precedent: Britbox, the new UK streaming service, already charges for vintage BBC shows. Ministers may nonetheless be tempted to hesitate: why not let the corporation stew in its own juice until it begs for release? Sadly, by then it may be too late. Let's hope Boris can get this one done.

A longer version of this piece appeared in the February issue of Standpoint.

About the contributor

David Cox is a television producer and writer on media. He has made programmes for ITV, the BBC and Channel 4, mainly about current affairs and history, and was head of current affairs at London Weekend Television for five years. He has written about broadcasting for the *New Statesman*, *Prospect*, *Standpoint*, the *Guardian* and the *London Evening Standard*.

Chapter 5

The causes of the BBC's real and present danger

The BBC remains a vital guardian of Britain's cultural life, which no politician should be allowed to imperil says Gillian Reynolds

The BBC's very real and present peril springs from three causes, the current government, changing communications technology and the BBC itself.

No British government in living memory has declared such open hostility towards its longest established broadcaster as Boris Johnson's has. Furthermore, that hostility extends to any part of the press that questions its policies. Refusal of access to anyone likely to disagree with Johnson would have been unthinkable a mere year ago.

Amazingly, we put up with it. It's only Boris, we say. It's not Hitler's Germany, Stalin's Russia, Mao's China or Trump's America. Well, now we know. It's suddenly become more like all of them and almost before anyone has noticed. Prime Minister Johnson now not only boycotts mainstream media but threatens the BBC by setting up an enquiry into its funding, one which could enrich press and new media competitors but significantly reduce consumer choice.

The BBC's head on a platter

There have been many previous enquiries into the funding of the BBC, usually hostile. All, eventually, have endorsed the licence fee. Subscription has been advocated as an alternative for at least four decades. This time it will be different, partly because communications technology has changed, mostly because Johnson wants delivery of the BBC's head. The BBC, so far, seems mainly to be debating how much parsley should deck the platter.

BBC chairman Sir David Clementi has rejected the notion of "Netflix-style" subscription, claiming it would imperil valued services. But anyone who uses the BBC knows it has already, and almost unnoticed, stepped towards a form of agreed access by requesting 'sign-ins' for iPlayer and 'subscriptions' to BBC Sounds.

So far, at no charge. Yet for all his threats that subscription would imperil BBC news and probably chop regional broadcasting, local radio and children's programmes, the chairman will know how the BBC could survive. It holds data that could enable it to put its content behind a paywall should the new government inquiry recommend it. Added to that, it is also already a Netflix-style co-producer of hit TV shows. Stepping further into the international co-production market could, if well enough managed, bridge the gap between the BBC set up as the British Broadcasting Company in 1922 and a BBC of the future as a brand recognized and trusted throughout the English-speaking world.

The original company was designed to be funded by its users: radio listeners. It cost ten shillings (50p in today's money) for a licence. According to Asa Briggs's 1979 history of the BBC, over half a million people bought one in 1922, over a million the next year, and by 1939 there were almost nine million. When black and white BBC television became national in the early 1950s the licence fee duly embraced it, again as a monopoly. That TV monopoly was broken in 1955, radio's in 1973.

Newspapers have sought throughout to protect their interests by attacking the BBC and its public funding. As broadcasting established itself and opportunities to profit from it grew, so did the protests from rivals against the BBC's guaranteed licence fee income. Hence all the government inquiries, from 1923 to now.

The shifting centre of technological gravity

Subscription has been suggested as an alternative since the 1980s. The BBC has always fought against it – politically, diplomatically, vigorously, cannily – to protect its own interests. For the most part, it has won. Now it's different. The broadcast age is ending. The world is online. The BBC started shifting its own centre of technological gravity towards online quite early, funded mostly by licence fee income but partly from its own commercial interests. Online is international. The BBC's rivals are now global businesses with the means to fund immense ventures in both technology and content. One big question facing the BBC is, if it survives, how British it can remain.

A symbol of Britishness – but for how long?

Once it existed to broadcast principally to speakers of English. English is now international. The BBC, after the Queen, remains the most recognized international symbol of the UK. Licence fee income now also funds the BBC World Service, a duty transferred to it in the agreement before last, later augmented by subventions from the Foreign Office in recognition of

World Service's massive international significance. World Service radio, in both English and its many other language services, is the global champion brand, continuing to grow in both listenership and reputation.

In the domestic market, against strong competition, BBC radio still commands just under half the audience. What does BBC radio supply on a scale rivals cannot, or wouldn't want to?

- News – national, international and local. Radio is still where people turn first for news.
- Sport – although competition for rights has reduced some BBC coverage. sport remains a major source of information and reference.
- Music – the BBC offers every kind, live or on record, significant support of new artists, established orchestras and musical education at every level.
- Drama, fiction and poetry – without licence fee income the supply of all of them would be severely limited.

Does that matter? It does. Who supported Tom Stoppard through a long dry spell and helped Lee Hall become a professional writer? The BBC radio drama department. Anyone with a pennyworth of sense knows that if the subscription were to be wholly voluntary the BBC would be out of business by the end of the decade.

What would be lost? Jobs. Talent. But the corporation no longer trains and retains staff. Heads of department lack their erstwhile autocracy. BBC trainees who became famous creatives (Armando Iannucci, for one) won't tolerate the BBC bureaucracy now involved in getting a programme on air. BBC TV began as one channel, expanded to two, then four but gave one up to online and now has scarcely enough original material to fill the remaining three. Cuts to radio budgets have slashed original output over the past three years. Look at the schedules. Count the repeats.

Sound as a pound?

Yet BBC radio still makes every pound go further. All its networks – national, regional, local, digital – plus podcasts, can now be found on BBC Sounds, replacement for the radio iPlayer. As every listener knows we are constantly being shepherded towards BBC Sounds for much of this, whether live or as podcasts.

Sounds is a massive investment. How big? Outsiders can't tell because Sounds appears in the BBC Annual Report as part of 'digital', not radio. Yet the current intent is that Sounds should, sooner rather than later, replace broadcast radio. If subscription turns out to be what this latest inquiry recommends then Sounds is the long sought-after route to it for BBC radio. That kind of BBC radio will not be as various as the broadcast networks we know now.

Overall, competition in broadcast radio remains fierce, mainly for the big audiences music brings. Not classical music. Classic FM makes a living in the commercial field, Scala has made a tentative start. Both exist within Britain's two big radio groups, Global and Bauer, each owning multiple stations broadcasting every kind of pop from the 60s to now. News Corp, owners of The Times and The Sunday Times, also own the Wireless Group which embraces music station Virgin alongside talkRADIO and talkSPORT. Soon it will launch Times Radio, with the aim of amortising the talent pool and cost of its market leading newspapers. That may take time. LBC, Britain's first legal commercial station, now part of the Global group and a vigorous competitor with the BBC, just announced a record audience share of 2.6 per cent. BBC Radio 4 has 12 per cent.

Radio 3 helps keep alive the UK's whole musical life, opera to rap, and is now the only place you'll hear a whole play by Shakespeare, Shaw or Sheridan. Radio 1 and Radio 2 support new artists on a scale unmatched. Radio 4 broadcasts more new plays to bigger audiences in one day than the National Theatre does in a year. If its comedy just now is not exactly in blossom, be patient.

Articles of faith

What the BBC really needs if it to survive the next decade is faith. In itself, its role in national life. In holding politicians to account. In its capacity to spot and develop talent. In offering all employees fair and equal pay. In its value in the world. To be able to do any of that it needs a realistic assessment of its current assets and shortcomings, one to which its employees as well as its customers are allowed to contribute.

The BBC needs advocacy. Informed, serious, persuasive advocacy. Whoever succeeds Tony Hall as director-general must not only have the ability to face down agents asking giant fees for unremarkable clients but the courage to tell the government the value of the BBC as a national and international asset.

Rumours persist that Hall is in the process of hiving off the Proms to a separate educational trust. Let us hope they are not true. The Proms, even on 90 per cent seat sales, will always show a balance sheet loss. The licence fee covers that loss, a debt worth paying if it underscores the survival of music in schools and concert halls all over the UK.

James Purnell, Hall's director of education and radio, recently told the Association of British Orchestras that he wants "to help audiences develop a lifelong love of classical music". Where has he been? Perhaps he's forgotten the listeners deprived of *Friday Night is Music Night* because Sounds has robbed the Radio 2 programme bank. Still, only the BBC offers every kind of music. Ditto comedy. Ditto drama. Ditto politics.

Netflix or Amazon can't do that. It's not their job. It is the BBC's. No prime minister on the rampage should make that job impossible. No chairman should let him. And every BBC licence fee-payer has a right to a voice in the debate.

About the contributor

Gillian Reynolds is The Sunday Times' radio critic having held the same role at The Telegraph for 42 years and The Guardian for seven. She was the first woman programme controller of a commercial radio station, running Radio City in Liverpool, which is now part of Bauer Group.

Chapter 6

Time to face up and front up for the BBC

Once one of its fiercest critics in Parliament, Rob Wilson, the former minister and MP for Reading East, is no less vociferous now he is out of Westminster

The British Broadcasting Corporation is a 20th century construct trying to survive in the fast-paced digital world of the 21st century. Its governance, its management, decision-making structure and its culture are no longer fit for purpose – there are very few in the business community who would question that the BBC's operating model is outdated and woefully inadequate.

If all its enormous corporate challenges were not enough on their own to overcome, it has also failed to convince the public that the BBC can be trusted. It has therefore failed to convince licence fee-payers that it can fulfil one of its core responsibilities: to remain impartial. A devastating failure for a publicly funded broadcaster.

Licence fee = poll tax?

Unsurprisingly, many viewers have felt for a long time that the BBC licence fee, effectively a poll tax on television use, is unfair. Poll after poll for over a decade has confirmed that most of the public want it scrapped, with around three quarters supporting abolition in the most recent one (Public First poll – January 2020). The lowest support is with 18-24-year-olds, many of whom rarely watch television. The media industry has changed, with the digital era enabling choice through a subscription model to become the norm.

It began with Sky, developed with Netflix and now Disney and others are piling in – by comparison making the BBC look old, stodgy, both out of its depth and out of date. The BBC's chances of competing successfully without a huge increase in funding are very slim to non-existent.

Is the BBC biased?

The business challenge for the BBC would itself cause a huge headache even for the country's best business brains, but the situation worsens when it is combined with the recent raw Brexit politics of the UK. There are regularly accusations of political bias thrown at the BBC and its news output (sometimes its entertainment as well). Indeed, ITV News is now more trusted as an impartial source of news than the BBC, better reflecting what is going on in the country (Savanta ComRes poll). Whilst politicians are thrown into a rage by some perceived slight or bias with great regularity, it is also true that, when assessed by experts, there is an issue. But not of overt political bias, it is much more a bias towards a metropolitan outlook that is largely out of touch with swathes of the country.

The BBC has absorbed into its DNA a world view. which is reflected in the people it employs and their desire to reflect these very liberal views. The BBC then presses these on to its licence fee payers without any consultation or notion of consent – causing the festering discontent. The BBC is largely out of touch with those that fund it.

Where is the BBC going?

Where does an organisation go next with its paying customers when it has eroded their trust and acted in bad faith in breaching their consent? That's not to suggest that the BBC does not have some fine talent and some great programmes which the public love – with an income of well over £5bn annually it should have. It also does not mean that there are not superb BBC journalists and commentators, there are plenty. There is also residual trust in the BBC's news output at times of crisis, during big international events or national occasions. But not enough and it will not hold back the tide of economic, business, social and political forces lining up against the BBC.

Has the BBC adapted?

Under Lord Hall, the BBC did try to make some important changes and to edge its way beyond its 20th century culture. BBC Store, iPlayer and BBC Sounds were all important digital investments to try to compete with the likes of iTunes and Netflix. Its new BritBox streaming service partnership with ITV will help it to financially mine its programme archive. However, the finance produced remains a gnat on an elephant when compared to the likes of iTunes and Netflix. Netflix alone will invest £12bn in programming this year and has around 140 million subscribers. Without radical new commercial freedoms, that it is extremely unlikely to get whilst charging a licence fee, the BBC has lost the economic battle with its competition before it has even begun.

Follow the money...

The BBC, charging £154.50 (and rising), currently raises over £3.5bn from the licence fee each year. Around a further £1.5bn is generated in revenue by its wholly owned international commercial arm BBC Studios. Whilst it might make sense for the BBC's commercial arm to do more to raise money by selling the corporation's content across the world, questions are already being posed as to why BBC licence fee payers should pay twice for content. New paid-for (subscription) services like BritBox will inevitably raise further objections about the BBC's financial model.

Does the BBC try to do too much? Does it do some of it badly?

There is also long-standing concern over the BBC's 'mission-creep'. If the BBC wants to introduce more iTunes-style charging or part-subscription services, it should not — and more to the point should not be allowed to — expand ever further into areas that could be provided by other media companies or private sector businesses. It is therefore unlikely that a licence fee-funded organisation will be able to generate sufficient income from other sources quickly enough to replace a sudden loss of fee income.

The BBC would not therefore be able to adjust to an abrupt change of funding model. The current government will need to give further consideration as to how highly it values the projection by the BBC of the nation's soft power around the world. Most governments have highly valued the BBC's reputation and the impact the BBC World Service has had in myriad of countries. Its loss would be a blow to the UK's influence.

The BBC has had a procession of disgraces and disasters over the past 10 years that it has survived. But there is currently a government in power that views change as inevitable. The notion that the BBC Charter and the licence fee system can continue with tinkering is not in government thinking. For all the reasons stated – technology, economics, business and management – change is coming and should have been driven by the BBC. Its management has been too wedded to the easy life that comes with enforced payments.

If the government's threat to decriminalise non-payment of the license fee in the courts goes through, it makes any enforcement of the licence fee impossible. The BBC estimates it will immediately take £200 million from its fee income. Although the BBC would be expected to make such claims, it is true that many who object to payment will simply refuse to pay, leaving a huge hole in BBC income and no way to plan spending on programmes and projects with any certainty.

The danger to the BBC is clear and obvious.

Where does the BBC go from here?

But all big organisations need an element of danger to be at their best. The BBC should not have been protected for so long from the cold, harsh world of commercial reality. It is right that a reckoning is finally here. So, where does the BBC go from here? The BBC would be wise to come forward with ideas, a consultation and agreement for a transition to a new funding model that the government can support. It desperately needs to be more in touch with and understand license fee payers.

My medicine for the BBC

There are several potential models or hybrid solutions:

a. A move to an entirely subscription model like Netflix or Amazon Prime
b. A co-operative ownership model, where those who pay a fee get to become owners of the organisation with consultation and decision-making rights
c. A move to a digital charging system for online downloads, much like iTunes
d. A BBC that is primarily subscription but with a small licence fee to fund a core of public service broadcasting, such as the provision of authoritative, impartial and comprehensive news reporting, and a strong educational element
e. A hybrid combination of elements that could involve freezing or reducing the licence fee from 2022, encouraging a switch to digital charging for services

All the options would result in a more narrowly-focused BBC – which is a good thing as it would not just be of benefit to taxpayers, but would foster a healthier, more diverse and more sustainable media sector in the UK. After all, the BBC already accounts for over 50 per cent of the average British person's consumption of news and current affairs across all media (Ofcom). Rupert Murdoch's media empire at its peak would have envied such audience penetration. It is too great a share for an organisation whose news output is not as trusted as it should be.

Monopoly and monopsony

In other markets such dominance would be considered monopolistic. The BBC has aggressively expanded its digital news and current affairs in recent years. The BBC should in future accept a limitation to its ambition, with all media organisations accepting a cap of around 25/30 per cent of market share across newspapers, broadcasting companies and websites. This would help to create a much healthier media sector, end the dominance of the BBC in news and current affairs, and allow new voices into the market.

The choices facing the BBC

The BBC is now in the long overdue position where it must make choices about its future. No doubt these choices have already been argued over internally and probably fiercely for the last decade – and all the while the industry has changed around it. The corporate sector is littered with much-loved and admired companies that failed to move with the times.

Poor management and untimely decision-making in a moribund 20th century structure have left the future of the BBC at the mercy of others. Make sensible decisions and choices now and the BBC can seek the time and the space to adapt and reform. Stick rigidly to its past and the licence fee model and the BBC's future may not be much of a future at all. The management of the BBC needs to demonstrate courage, boldness and leadership over the next decade otherwise it could be its last, and deservedly so.

About the contributor

Rob Wilson was the Conservative MP for Reading East from 2005-2017, and was Minister for Civil Society in the Cabinet Office from 2014-2017. He has published two books on politics.

Chapter 7

Life after the end of the licence fee

The licence fee is bound to go. Owen Bennett-Jones argues BBC managers should start planning now for what will come after it. Only then will they be able to preserve the best aspects of the BBC and ensure a future for independent broadcast journalism

The doomed licence fee

As the BBC contemplates future perils, it would help clarify matters if there was general agreement that the licence fee is unsustainable. Senior BBC managers privately concede this is the case but still find it difficult to contemplate life without it. The prospect of raising nearly £4bn year through another method is daunting.

There are a number of inescapable reasons why the licence fee will have to go. Increasing numbers believe the BBC to be – according to taste – statist, corporatist, elitist or liberal. This is no doubt part of a general trend of disenchantment in major institutions including Parliament but, for the BBC, it has especially profound implications. Historically, its best defence against hostile governments was the high levels of trust it enjoyed – typically around 70 per cent. The latest polling suggests that number won't be achieved again. A YouGov poll in December 2019 found that less than half of Britons now trust the BBC to tell the truth[1].

Disenchantment with the BBC and scepticism about its impartiality is not evenly spread. Back in the 1970s the BBC was most strongly opposed by the Left. Radical trades unionists and some on the fringes of the Labour Party complained that the organisation did not give sufficient space to the concerns of the majority of licence fee payers: the workers. Those voices still exist, but are now outnumbered by rightists who echo and even outdo the Corbynistas arguing that the BBC reflects a London-centric, out of touch elite. The right-winger's grievances are made all the more acute by their awareness that, with the newspapers so heavily tilted towards the Right, it is only the BBC that offers a substantial voice offering different perspectives. Today Brexiteers are the most distrustful of the BBC followed by Conservatives, Labour supporters and Liberals in that order.

The looming battle over decriminalisation

With the real possibility of a decade of Conservative government ahead, those figures look important. Even if the Conservatives hesitate to launch an all-out attack on the BBC, they are almost certain to pursue a war of attrition. After the free licence fees for over 75-year-olds, the next battle looks set to be decriminalisation of non-payment of the licence fee. From the point of view of the Johnson administration, a showdown with the liberal elite as represented by the BBC has many upsides. It could simultaneously please corporate competitors such as Murdoch, frighten BBC editors into being ever more cautious, and attract public support, not least with the Conservatives' new voters in the north. In the recent past the public could have been expected to rally to the BBC's defence to frustrate such a policy. But when people want their version of the truth reflected in the media they consume, it leaves the BBC vulnerable.

The young are streaming away from the BBC

The deteriorating political context is just one of the BBC's problems. It is also up against some difficult numbers. Last October, Ofcom reported that the BBC is reaching fewer people through TV, radio and the main online services, a trend which is most marked among 18 to 24 year olds, who are migrating to YouTube and Netflix[2]. The increasing competition from streaming services will make it all but impossible for the BBC to keep hold of the 90 per cent-plus audience share generally accepted as a being required to justify charging virtually everyone in the UK a flat rate fee. By the time 20 per cent of Brits are not consuming the BBC, it will be next to impossible to argue that everyone should continue to pay for it. Furthermore, the BBC's new competitors exist because of new technology that impacts the corporation in other ways. The BBC may have embraced digital with more flexibility than most state broadcasters but there is no escaping the anachronistic nature of a charge based on possession of a TV set at a time when increasing numbers access content through other means and screens.

So, for all these reasons, the licence fee will eventually have to go. How long that might take is the subject of worried conversations in the BBC's management corridors but most would probably give it no more than 15 years and in the light of the Johnson victory maybe less. In any event, BBC managers should start thinking now about alternatives, asking questions such as: what aspects of the BBC will be lost when the licence fee ends? What can be preserved? And can anything be gained?

The BBC's formidable commercial potential

Not so long ago the BBC's defenders relied on the claim that its demise would jeopardise nationally important and culturally significant dramas. But with Netflix now lavishing money on such productions, that argument no longer applies. And anyway, there are bigger issues to consider, the most significant being the threat to universality. The BBC's obligation to reach out to all segments of the British population in pursuit of its 90 per cent-plus audience contributes to national unity. And it's impossible to see how any other funding arrangement would preserve this aspect of the BBC's work. Having said that, the BBC's massive audience includes the people advertisers most want to reach – when the BBC is forced to raise its own revenue, whether it be through advertising, subscription or any other method, it has the potential to be a formidable commercial player, posing a significant challenge to existing commercial broadcasters. And it has an archive Netflix can only dream of. For these reasons it should be possible for the BBC to ensure that quality programmes remain intact. The day may come when the BBC can once again afford to buy the most attractive sports rights.

There are other possible gains from the changes that are coming. The BBC News operation is currently so big that it has an unhealthy monopolistic power and, when it comes to employment of journalists, a monopsony that restricts competition. Furthermore, the licence fee suits the politicians very well: it is sufficiently distinct from straight forward government funding via a departmental budget to enable them to assert that the BBC is free of government control, a claim that the BBC is keen to echo. And yet it is the same politicians who every few years get to decide whether the licence fee should remain in place and at what level it should be set. The idea that this does not give them influence over the output contradicts the universally accepted principle that whoever determines an institution's income gets what she or she wants.

The BBC as a state-run broadcaster

The consequence is a deep editorial caution that has long imbued the BBC's news judgments. Invisible red lines prevent BBC journalists from confronting the issues of greatest sensitivity to the UK's deep state. This is not new. One of the greatest tests for the BBC's independence was Northern Ireland: when the conflict there was at its height, BBC journalists who went off-script were dismissed. And as recently as 2014, the BBC's then monitoring service in Caversham was generating material for the British intelligence services that was not made available to most BBC journalists. The BBC thereby revealed itself to be what a state-funded channel must always be. Not like its Russian or Iranian counterparts, maybe, but a state-run channel nonetheless. It's difficult to argue that faced with another challenge as testing as that presented by the IRA, the BBC's managers would have the courage to act in a genuinely independent way.

What does the future hold?

There is consequently the possibility that if the transition to new funding arrangements were well managed, there could be a new phase of genuinely independent broadcast journalism. Many of the BBC's supporters – including most of its staff – are more fearful of the future than hopeful. They argue that, as it stands, the BBC offers a source of reliable fact-checked information at a time when such output is more needed than ever. When a significant number of people don't believe, for example, that vaccinations work, a major media platform which can insist with authority that they do, brings real benefits to society.

But change is coming and those running the BBC need to make the best of it. For a successful transition to a new future, managers need to start planning now. They are far more likely to preserve the best things about the BBC and secure a future for independent journalism if they go on the front foot now and start shaping their own future rather than let someone else determine the outcome. In all likelihood, however, the BBC will cling on to the licence fee for as long as possible until an alternative is forced upon it. And that is where the real peril lies.

About the contributor

Owen Bennett-Jones is a freelance journalist and writer who presented Newshour on the BBC World Service and was a foreign correspondent in Geneva, Bucharest, Hanoi, Beirut and Islamabad. He has taught at Princeton University and the University of Southern California, and is the author of a forthcoming book on the Bhutto dynasty to be published by Yale University Press.

References

1.   Available online at https://yougov.co.uk/topics/politics/articles-reports/2019/12/16/do-britons-trust-press Date accessed: 3 February 2020.

2. Available online at https://www.ofcom.org.uk/tv-radio-and-on-demand/information-for-industry/bbc-operating-framework/performance/bbc-annual-report. Date accessed: 3 February 2020.

Chapter 8

There is opportunity amid the existential threat to the BBC

Many of the challenges facing the BBC are familiar, believes Richard Sambrook, but a lack of relevance to the under-30 audience is sharpening the existential danger, and a clear plan is urgently required

The BBC faces a hostile government seeking to end the licence fee in favour of advertising. Meanwhile, political polarisation has undermined consensus about its role, it faces increased competition and technology is rapidly changing viewing habits. And there is serious criticism of its editorial performance.

I am not talking about today – although all of the above apply – but the mid 1980s when the Thatcher government set up the Peacock Committee to report on the BBC's finances with the expectation it would recommend advertising. Meanwhile home video recording was presenting challenges to viewer numbers and there was fierce public controversy led by government over its coverage of Northern Ireland.

The BBC responded by promoting finance director Michael Checkland to director-general and bringing in former London Weekend Television boss John Birt as his deputy and anointed successor. The Peacock Committee decided the licence fee was "the least worst option" for funding, so it survived. Checkland started a series of radical internal reforms, continued by Birt, who introduced specialist journalism and more rigour into news and oversaw a major investment in news and current affairs. He also – with great intuition and foresight – developed new channels and online services which enabled the BBC to expand and develop its public service role into the digital age.

With Tony Hall stepping down as director-general, many commentators are rightly identifying this as a key moment for the BBC. It faces huge challenges in terms of political support, issues over its funding, competition from new platforms and services and a questioning of its role in a fractured social environment. But it would be wrong to conclude that its path ahead is only downhill.

Hall leaves a significant legacy. He steadied the organisation after the revelations about the crimes of sexual predator Jimmy Savile forced another director-general, George Entwistle, to resign. He successfully negotiated a ten-year charter and new licence fee settlement providing future stability, he secured greater investment in the World Service. As a modernising force, he further developed iPlayer, launched BBC Sounds, Britbox and BBC Studios, helping the organisation adapt with the rapidly evolving competition for on-demand content and a global rights market. But he leaves with, once again, questions about the longevity of the licence fee, the BBC's impartiality in a divided society, significant savings still to be delivered (on top of some 20 per cent over the last decade) and the shadow of Apple, Amazon, Netflix, Disney and others cast over the smaller commissioning budgets for British content.

The morale-sapping sore of pay inequality

Hall's successor faces a formidable array of challenges. First, there are at least two running issues to resolve. The last licence fee deal accepted responsibility for free licences for the over-75s. But as that responsibility is about to transfer from government to the corporation they have said only those means-tested should qualify. The impact of free licences for all over-75s would be equivalent to the costs of BBC2, BBC3, BBC4, BBC News Channel and CBBC and CBeebies combined – in other words, unmanageable. But the new Conservative government has not yet accepted the BBC's position. In terms of budgets, this is a huge issue to resolve – one that a previous director general, Mark Thompson, was prepared to resign over rather than accept.

Then there are the running disputes over equal pay. The BBC, in common with many other large organisations, allowed a significant pay gap to establish itself between male and female staff and presenters. It has been slow to resolve this and there are a series of potentially damaging tribunals waiting to be scheduled. This is a morale-sapping sore that needs healing rapidly. Then there are the more structural issues. Like many parts of the media, the BBC is searching for ways to fully engage the under-30 audience who are less loyal and spend less time in front of TV. There have been plenty of creative attempts to fashion programming for them, including BBC3, but as yet insufficient traction as an Ofcom report in October 2019 noted. The lack of interest in the BBC by the future audience is, obviously, an existential issue.

Technology continues to develop, transforming consumer habits and expectations. The BBC has been traditionally bold with new technology – the first major UK news website, iPlayer as the first UK on-demand service – but there is a sense that it is falling behind as bigger global organisations invest harder. Hall recognised that on-demand audio and video was the future. The challenge is the pace of transition – how to serve current audience needs while moving towards a very different model for future audiences. The BBC needs a fresh and clear vision of what it should do and how swiftly.

And finally there is the political challenge. The BBC emerged from the general election with few friends on any side in Westminster, and with a government limbering up to question the licence fee and core purpose of the organisation. Thompson, speaking on the Andrew Marr programme in January 2020, was right to say that if subscription is introduced the BBC will be a very successful, smaller broadcaster – but it will not be the BBC any more. Universality – providing public service content for all, not just those that can afford it – is the corporation's core purpose.

An antidote to fake news and disinformation

But as it faces increased competition from global giants there is also opportunity. The BBC is the only global media brand the UK has. The World Service continues to be successful and popular. Set against American media giants, the BBC is a minnow – but one with a strong brand and creative record that still allows it to compete. In promoting the UK around the world, the BBC can be a valuable asset in post-Brexit Britain. And in times of weak trust, fake news and disinformation its commitment to fairness and accuracy (setting aside contrary views on how well it delivers that) can be a major asset in pulling the country back together.

With growing inequality of access to quality content the case for public service media should be strong. So in huge challenges, there is also opportunity. The new director-general will need strategic vision, political acumen, significant managerial experience and the constitution to implement difficult, painful, radical change in the face of constant political and public criticism. It is probably the toughest job in UK media and also the most important.

This article first appeared in theconversation.com on 21 January 2020

About the contributor

Richard Sambrook is Professor of Journalism at Cardiff University and director of its Centre for Journalism. He was a journalist for 30 years at BBC News, including ten years on the board of management as Director of Sport, Director of News and Director of Global News. He has also been global vice chairman of communications firm Edelman, where he was a consultant on media to numerous global organisations. He has been a visiting fellow at the Reuters Institute of Journalism at the University of Oxford.

Chapter 9

Is its news operation the chink in the BBC's armour?

To ensure that the BBC has a future, is the only solution for the corporation to end its endlessly troublesome news output, along with the pretence that due impartiality is achievable? Brian Winston and Matthew Winston ponder that question

By 1926, George V had noticed something:

> *More than two million persons in our Kingdom of Great Britain and Northern Island have applied for and taken out Licences to install and operate apparatus for wireless telegraphy for the purpose of receiving broadcast programmes.*[1]

These pioneering millions, the charter we have just been quoting states, were listening with "widespread interest" to limited programming provided by a company owned by the manufacturers of the apparatuses – 'wirelesses' as they were already being called by 1904, or 'radios' (as the Americans would have it from 1915). Its "Service" was deemed by the king (or whoever wrote these things for him) to be "of great value… as a means of education and entertainment".

The transmitting company providing the programming was not the creation of an early 20th-century entrepreneur. Rather, the entity was a creature of His Majesty's Post-Master General, a politician with a seat at the cabinet table, who had forced the manufacturers into a partnership in order to create it. From the start of 1923 until the end of 1926, the PMG licensed it to broadcast to the listeners, whom he had also licensed to listen.

As the end-date approached, the king, bless him, deemed it desirable that "the Service should be developed and exploited to the best advantage and in the national interest" and so, by his "special grace, certain knowledge and mere motion", he nationalised the company. As of 1 January 1927, it was replaced by a "corporation" with its own board of governors, licensed by the P-MG to be the monopoly provider of "British Broadcasting" for the next ten years.

The BBC charter – a royal jewel

There is no better or more succinct account of the fate of this Royal Charter, renewed and amended over the decades since the twenties, than the BBC's own official historian, Professor Jean Seaton. She calls the document the "jewel in the crown" in the little internet lecture on it you can find on the web.[2] Bullet-point by bullet-point, she indicates the salient issues addressed in these more or less decadal extensions and amendments to it, and to the more detailed practical agreement document that goes with it.

A key iteration was the 1964 version, which absorbed the abandonment of the monopoly with the arrival of commercial television, established by the Television Act of 1954. Seaton, however, picks out the 1975 amendment as critical. By "mere motion" (as it were), this transferred responsibility from the P-MG to the Home Secretary. The move facilitated interference in content and, over the next 45 years, subsequent repeated changes to the corporation's relationship to the state came to constitute what Seaton describes as "muggings". By 2016, the BBC found itself subject to the attentions of Ofcom, which had absorbed the P-MG's functions. Its hands were already full with its responsibilities regulating commercial broadcasters, new digital platforms, the post and telecoms generally. But now it has to find time to offer the corporation "guidance on contents".[3]

Thomas Jefferson warned that all states "have propensities to command at will the liberty…. of their constituents", an observation true of even the liberal representative democracies.[4] The "propensity" became an obligation with radio, initially a military technology, because it required state allocation of bandwidth if it was to be effectively diffused as a mass-medium. That allocative function, of course, says nothing as to the matter of "guidance on contents", nor does the question of the receivers' licence fees, either. This hypothecated tax, which can of course be justified in the name of 'education and entertainment' -- certainly at a minimum for making good marketplace deficiencies with the later – in not the problem. Neither technology nor tax are the source of the BBC's problems. Although criminalising non-payment of the tax is no help, that is a minor factor in the existential threat. The irresistible governmental "propensities" to interfere, in ways hostile to the principles of the free press, are at the root of the crisis.

Why? We need to return to the original charter and, as a clue, note the significant omission of one word: news.

It is no accident that the charter omits mention of news. This is not because news wasn't being broadcast. It was, from the off. There was entertainment; music both popular and classical -- even, experimentally, in 1922, before the company's founding. *Children's Hour* was also on air. The quarrel scene between Cassius and Brutus in Shakespeare's *Julius Caesar* was broadcast early in 1923. That same year an educational department was established. And there were news bulletins provided by the press.

In all this there was a certain amount of friction with the established media, arising from a perceived threat of competition. Artists' contracts, for example, soon came to include clauses restricting appearance on the wireless, and the press was particularly hostile. No news could be broadcast until the last edition of the evening papers had hit the streets. The government was well aware of, and sensitive to, these other interests. It is not as if the king woke up one morning in 1926 and dictated the BBC's charter. In fact, there had been two committees of inquiry, in 1923 and 1926, both of which spent much time addressing the worries of the stage, the music business and the press – as well as consulting with religious and educational bodies. It is in response that both came to recommend the establishment of a sole public-owned national programming organisation, with its own independent management as, in part, a way of assuaging these concerns.[5]

News – the chink in the armour

It is possible to read the history of the BBC as an object lesson in how fragile 'independence' is, when it is graciously granted by the state in such a manner. But although there are endless curtain-twitching brouhahas about sex and violence and how the sound is too loud etc etc, the bottom line is that if the charter is the jewel in the crown, then the news is the chink in the armour. Dominic Cummings' tastes in programming are not known, but his hostility to the BBC as an organ of news and opinion is. Ditto every politician who has ever seriously questioned the corporation's programming. It's never the asinine game shows or the repeated adaptions of the same classic novels. It's always the news.

The incidents are ever-better known. Before the charter even came into effect, the BBC had moved its news operation into government offices in order to 'independently' cover the 1926 General Strike.[6] For decades a chap from MI5 sat vetting sensitive appointments (largely, of course, in news and current affairs) in an office in Broadcasting House.[7] And at all moments of national crisis and division the BBC has had to struggle, almost always in secret, to report the news. It is remarkable in such circumstances that it should have achieved a reputation for journalistic integrity sufficient to worry the politicians.[8]

The ideology of the BBC incorporates some touchingly naive articles of faith when it comes to the news. It believes, it seems, that it can produce news impartially – with 'due impartiality', even. It can't, and the repeated dancing on the head of a pin involved in pretending otherwise (e.g. you can say on-air that a tweet is racist, but you can't call the tweeter racist, to take the latest notorious incident)[9] proves the impossibility. The BBC also believes it has conventions to protect it, though clearly nobody has told Dominic Cummings. It has thought in the past to approach the periodic charter-renewal processes as an equal negotiating partner with the government. It isn't. Another nurses the illusion that if it is attacked for bias both from right and left, that proves it to be neutral, but in fact the charges, incident by incident, could all be well-founded, and this is no defence at all. But now this game appears to be up.

One solution is to remove the chink in the armour. A key journalistic objective is – as Marchamont Needham, Cromwell's PR-man and a father of the English press, put it – "the tearing down of vizards, veils and disguises".[10] The BBC, as a tax-funded institution, is in no position to do that vis-à-vis the state that sustains it. Lose the news and, as the 1927 charter indicated, education and entertainment are left intact. Keep the news and it, education and entertainment, are all threatened.

Or, if you really want to be fanciful, you could suggest that, in its second century, the charter tells, allocative functions aside, Ofcom and all the politicians to get lost (as with the press, the general law suffices). And the standard of due impartiality, assumed everywhere except in the BBC, correctly, to be impossible, should not be expected. The tax, too, could be set robotically in line with the cost of living index (or some such). Above all, though, it could state that it is as illegal to mess with content on air as it is to do so with the rest of the press.

But, of course, fat chance…

About the contributors

Brian Winston is the Lincoln Professor at the University of Lincoln. The Roots of Fake News, his next book (written with Matthew Winston) will be published by Routledge.

Matthew Winston teaches in the School of Media, Communication and Sociology at the University of Leicester. His Gonzo Text: Disentangling Meaning in Hunter S. Thompson's Journalism is published by Peter Lang.

Notes

1. The Royal Charter (20 December 1927). http://downloads.bbc.co.uk/bbctrust/assets/files/pdf/regulatory_framework/charter_agr eement/archive/1927.pdf accessed 14 February 2020].
2. Jean Seaton| *Jean Seaton, on the BBC Royal Charter* | BBC | 27 March 2017. https://www.bbc.co.uk/programmes/p04y61zf [accessed 14 February 2020].
3. See, for example: Anon (Ofcom) 2019. *Review of BBC news and current affairs*, 24 October. https://www.ofcom.org.uk/tv-radio-and-on-demand/information-for-industry/bbc-operating-framework/performance/review-bbc-news-current-affairs [accessed 14 February 2020].
4. Jefferson, Thomas (1787, [1782]) *Notes on the State of Virginia*. London: John Stockdale.
5. Briggs, Asa (1995). *The History of Broadcasting in the United Kingdom, Volume I: The Birth of Broadcasting* Oxford: Oxford University Press.
6. Briggs, Asa (1995). *The History of Broadcasting in the United Kingdom, Volume I: The Birth of Broadcasting* Oxford: Oxford University Press, pp. 152-157.
7. Reynolds, Paul (2018). 'The vetting files: How the BBC kept out "subversives"' *BBC News*, 22 April. https://www.bbc.co.uk/news/stories-43754737 [accessed 10 January 2020].
8. Thorpe, Vanessa (2020). 'Hostile politicians, cuts and controversy: why the BBC has never been so vulnerable', *The Observer*, 2 February, pp. 48/49.
9. Richard Spillett, 2019. 'Former BBC chairman MICHAEL GRADE sees trouble on the horizon following the Naga Munchetty 'racism' scandal'. *Mail Online* 2 October https://www.dailymail.co.uk/news/article-7524817/Lord-Grade-says-corporation-RIGHT-criticise-Naga-Munchetty.html [accessed 9 October 2019].
10. qt in Frank, Joseph (1961). *The Beginnings of the English Newspaper, 1620-1660*. Cambridge, Mass: Harvard University Press, p.59.

Chapter 10

The BBC will be different and smaller – but it must remain

While it might frustrate everyone from time to time, including him, corporation 'lifer' John Simpson argues that the BBC is a fragile organisation whose continued existence matters for audiences across the globe

It will probably be May before we know who has got the job as the BBC's next director-general. Whoever it is, they will have the BBC's future in their hands. And a single slip could see the entire, seemingly tough – yet actually rather fragile – outfit crash to the ground in a thousand pieces.

Would it matter? A lot of people, more now than ever before, will say 'no'. But as a BBC lifer – I joined as a junior sub-editor in 1966, and have worked in the news department ever since – you'll forgive me if I say I think it does matter immensely.

For almost a century it has done a pretty good job of enlightening us, informing us and entertaining us. The BBC has helped to make us who we are as a nation. It has provided us with a daily and hourly picture of ourselves and our world. There can scarcely be a man, woman or child in the entire United Kingdom who has not been affected by its broadcasting. It enrages all of us from time to time (me included), but those who can see the wider picture tend to support it as an institution, even when there are aspects of it that they don't like.

New director-general must contend with increased polarisation

The new BBC boss will be faced with a variety of problems greater than any previous DG has had to deal with. One of them is the undeniable fact that the widespread support the BBC has always relied on has been affected by the two hugely divisive issues we have faced over the past few years: Scottish independence and Brexit. The middle ground which the BBC had always inhabited suddenly disappeared; where, after all, is the middle ground between independence or remaining in the United Kingdom, or between staying in the EU or leaving it? People who had previously been perfectly rational started to detect bias in everything, from the tone of voice in a news bulletin to the audiences for *Question Time*. It didn't seem to matter that roughly similar numbers of people were detecting exactly the opposite bias at exactly the same time.

The December 2019 General Election made it even worse. Corbynistas were certain the BBC was obeying the instructions of the Conservative Campaign Headquarters (CCHQ) to destroy their man, at the very moment when CCHQ was incandescent at the BBC for what it saw as the Corporation's anti-Tory bias. Again and again, our presenters were accused of being unfair to one side or another, and we were regularly told we had failed to question the claims of the various parties. That was demonstrably untrue, since after the 2016 referendum the BBC set up a highly effective fact-checking department which broadcast its conclusions on a regular basis, and published them on the BBC's hugely popular website. But if people want to believe something, reality doesn't seem to stop them.

Personally, I'm not a great supporter of the argument that if you're upsetting everyone you must be getting it about right. All the same, you might hope that people who believe the BBC is cravenly obeying the will of the government might notice that other people are just as loud in claiming that the BBC is totally biased against the government.

So the first thing the next director-general will have to do is to rebuild its reputation for balance and neutrality. But there will be other pressing problems. Lord Hall is standing aside because he thinks the same person should negotiate the next BBC Charter, from 2027 onwards, and the upcoming licence fee deal.

Those are going to be two very difficult subjects, and there is no doubt that Boris Johnson, with his chief of staff Dominic Cummings whispering in his ear, is going to want to seem ultra-tough on the licence fee in particular. Many of the new Tory MPs who have taken their seats at Westminster are likely to be more populist and hard-line than their predecessors, and public support for the licence fee has been dropping fast.

There will be a great deal of horse-trading, playing off the licence fee against details of the next Charter, and the new director-general will have to keep his or her nerve. But what sort of BBC should emerge from all this? I suspect it will have to concentrate on its core activities – news, current affairs, factual programming, music for all tastes, high-quality series like *The Trial of Christine Keeler* and *Fleabag* – while letting Netflix and the other British channels concentrate on other entertainment.

The BBC will be different and smaller

My guess is that the licence fee will continue at a lower level – most other European countries have something like it, after all – but that people who want more than the basics will have to pay a top-up fee to watch them, much as they do with Sky or Netflix. The ace in the new director-general's hand will surely be that no government will want to go down in history as the one that destroyed the BBC.

Remember, 2022 will be the hundredth anniversary of the corporation's establishment, and any incoming director-general can be expected to play this up for all it's worth, showcasing for months on end how good the BBC has genuinely been over the years, and reminding us all how much we've got from it. Around the world, the BBC's reputation has rarely been higher – its audiences are just under half a billion now, and growing fast. It would be very foolish indeed to do too much damage to something as valuable as this.

In the years when Margaret Thatcher was prime minister, it was my job to follow her around the world. She would often sound off against the BBC, at press conferences or when I interviewed her. But she never forgot that most British people supported it. Immediately after her third election victory in 1987, I door-stepped her in front of a crowd of young Tories chanting: "Privatise the BBC!" After asking her a couple of questions, I said: "These people want you to privatise the BBC. You can do it now. Will you?"

"Well, I think…" she began, then said: "Oh look, there's Dennis. I must go and join him." That's it, I thought – she won't do it, and she never really intended to.

However radical Dominic Cummings wants to be now, I suspect that Boris Johnson's gut political instincts will mean he stops short of doing anything too damaging to the BBC. But that doesn't mean the next director-general won't have a pretty torrid time.

And I'm pretty sure that the BBC which takes shape after 2027 will be different – and quite a lot smaller – than the one all of us have known, all our lives.

This article first appeared in dailymail.co.uk *on 21 January 2020*

About the contributor

John Simpson is the BBC's World Affairs Editor, leading its team of foreign and special correspondents. He has worked for the corporation for more than 50 years, beginning his career in 1966. During that time he has reported from more than 100 countries, including 30 war zones. He has published a range of books based on his foreign reporting, including *A Mad World, My Masters* (2000) and *News from No Man's Land* (2002), as well as three novels. He has twice been named the Royal Television Society's Journalist of the Year.

Chapter 11

Don't make the BBC bow to the great god of commerce

Even if the licence fee were a conventional tax it would still be worth keeping, says Damian Reilly, who argues that Britain meddles with the BBC – the envy of the world – at its peril

I sometimes wonder if I'm the last person left in Britain who loves the BBC and thinks it represents brilliant value for money. Yes, there is much with which to be infuriated – like most Leavers, for example, I find watching Gary Lineker present *Match of the Day* about as enjoyable as I imagine Remainers would watching Nigel Farage do the same job. And yes, the *Today* programme segment I listened to yesterday on the latest developments in telephone hold music was idiotic. But does the BBC really deserve, once again, to be threatened with licence fee reform?

The argument against the BBC licence fee is that it is effectively a tax. It isn't – you can opt-out – but even if it were it would be a good thing. Our taxes are rightly spent on services many of which as individuals we will never use. But the BBC is a service almost all of us use, every day, and which genuinely is the envy of the world.

The BBC – the home of Blairite refugees

Yes, it seems now to be staffed, near exclusively, by gushing liberals and centrist Blairite refugees. But this is hardly surprising – nor such a bad thing. Gushing liberals are drawn more toward media careers than, say, science boffins, and it was ever thus. On the whole, they make better programmes than boffins, certainly when it comes to light entertainment. And the Blairite refugees are simply the overhanging reality of Beeb appointments made between the years of 1997 and 2007 when the prevailing national culture was defined by the New Labour credo.

No doubt when the pendulum finally swings back the other way and Labour returns to power, the public will find itself as at odds as it is now with decisions made by Beeb bosses appointed during the Cameron/Johnson/Cummings years. In that respect, BBC managers are like

Supreme Court judges, relics from a bygone era with the power to act as counterbalances. One suspects in 2035, QUESTION TIME panels stuffed with nation-state evangelists might seem as sinister and weird as does Shami Chakrabarti's near-ubiquity on the programme today. Probably, it all balances out in the end.

Holding back the race to the bottom

It's a point so obvious it barely needs stating, but what makes the BBC near ineffably precious as a cultural institution is its blessed freedom from chasing ratings. For thirty years, we have heard much moaning about the dumbing down of our culture. But who in good conscience thinks our culture is likely to get cleverer when the very thing that most forcibly shapes it is required to compete in the race to the bottom for eyeballs and ears? If you think MRS BROWN'S BOYS and TOP GEAR are don't-know-where-to-look bad now, just wait until there are subscription packages to be sold. And once the BBC is made to bow to the great god of commerce, then what next? People take to the streets to protest at the idea of our other great national miracle of civilisation, the NHS, being opened to even the smallest fraction to market forces. Why not then the same fear of upward pressure naturally being exerted on the cost of a BBC subscription? The service is meant to be for everyone – that's the whole point of it. No one should be priced out.

The story of the BBC

Every night, before they go to bed, my young children sit on our sofa with their warm milk and watch as a bedtime story is read to them by a celebrity on the CBeebies channel. It's a lovely, thoughtful piece of programming. As I look on, unfailingly I am struck by how heart-warming it is that, thanks to the BBC, every child in the land living in a home with a television has access to this simplest of a young life's pleasures – a story at the end of the day.

But, simultaneously, I am also struck by how at odds the programme is with the myriad lurid crash, bang, wallop cartoons – interspersed frequently with dementing adverts for expensive toys – being broadcast at the same time on the commercial channels offered by Sky. This disparity in output seems to me to encapsulate perfectly the radically different priorities of a genuine public service broadcaster to that of a business whose sole concern is getting people to cough up for its service every month. Of course, Sky could broadcast a similar programme to *CBeebies Bedtime Story*, but compared to bulk-bought cartoons, it would be expensive to create or to purchase, and so it doesn't.

The BBC's output is a product and it is right that those of us who consume it should pay for it. It is also right that no one should enjoy every piece of its programming. Almost certainly, too much of what is currently broadcast as entertainment by the BBC is overly politicised or produced seemingly with no higher concern than signifying the obeisance of the makers to liberal shibboleths of mindless progressivism. But that's a fad, and thankfully, it will soon pass, no doubt to be replaced in part by something else just as infuriating.

Auntie would be missed terribly

But for every boorish Nish Kumar on the BBC there is a Phoebe Waller-Bridge or a Russell T Davies. For every asinine Radio 4 Thought for the Day, there is a Jonathan Agnew sumptuously bringing to life a sporting event for whoever wants to listen, or a Mishal Husain holding some despot to account. In the rush to wallop Auntie at every available opportunity, this seems to be overlooked.

We should be very careful indeed with how we handle the BBC, because as a public service that is as brilliant as it is broad, it is irreplaceable. If we're stupid enough to wreck it, we will miss it terribly and it will be impossible to mend. That might not be fashionable to say these days, but it's the truth.

The original version of this article was published on The Spectator*'s website*

About the contributor

Damian Reilly is a freelance journalist who contributes to *The Spectator*, covering everything from politics and finance to sport.

Chapter 12

The BBC is biased but ...

Professor Ivor Gaber draws on his past experience as a BBC journalist to explain why the common accusations against the BBC of political bias are mistaken but, he argues, bias there is

The BBC is full of journalists doing their damnedest to broadcast unbiased news, of this I have no doubt about this – notwithstanding their having to bear the slings and arrows of outrageous, or outraged, politicians and their supporters denouncing 'Auntie' for her gross political bias.

But the outrage is now qualitatively different as BBC journalism finds itself sailing through much choppier waters than it did in the past when the worst of their critics amounted to either Harold Wilson complaining about a critical BBC documentary or Alec Douglas-Home saying the camera made his head look like a skull.

But, as the Johnson Government is now demonstrating, politics has become a far rougher trade especially as far as the BBC is concerned. This is partly because the Brexit debate created deep cleavages across, and within, parties and partly because the political divide between the two main parties has widened from being minuscule, when Blair and Cameron faced each other across the despatch boxes, to massive as Corbyn and Johnson stared each other down at their weekly PMQ jousts.

Having said all that in defence of the BBC, I do believe that an unconscious bias can be detected in the corporation's output – but bias not in the traditional sense of favouring the Right or the Left. The bias I am referring to manifests itself in three ways. First, there is the corporation's long-standing bias towards the political consensus; second there is the bias that emanates from it, and its staff's, generally homogenous position in society and, finally, there is the BBC's 'selfish gene' – its in-built survival instinct that leads it, perhaps justifiably, to treat rows with the Conservatives more seriously than it treats rows with the Labour Party.

All three were on display during the 2019 general election campaign. On one level it's difficult to recall a campaign that hasn't ended with both main parties accusing the BBC of biased reporting. The loudest complaints used to come from the losing party but in 2019 - as in 2015 – they came from the winners. Indeed, the Conservatives were so dissatisfied with the BBC's election coverage that they have instituted a boycott of some of the corporation's main political programmes and are threatening its future, both in terms of its funding and the scale of its operations. Whether this represents a serious undermining of our democracy, or just an attempt to undermine the BBC, is not yet clear; either way it is damaging.

Who bats for the BBC?

In these circumstances the BBC could usually count on the support of what might be termed liberal-left opinion but many on that side of the political divide are still licking their wounds, believing that their cause was not well-served by the BBC both during the Brexit referendum and then the 2019 election. And although there is still an unwavering commitment to preserving a strong public service broadcasting component in the UK's media environment, not everyone is now convinced that the BBC in its present form is the best model for achieving this.

So if both Left and Right and Leave and Remain supporters are critical of the BBC's coverage then 'job done' goes the clichéd argument – "If both/all sides are unhappy we must be getting the balance about right" old BBC hands used to opine. Thankfully we hear less of this specious argument these days.

In the past, furores about bias eventually died down and the BBC and the politicians rapidly got on with 'business as usual'. But things feel somewhat different today and that might well be partly a reflection of recent BBC failings and partly a reflection of the way our politics is now more polarised than at any time since the war.

The corporation's bias to the political consensus is a phenomenon long-noted by those who have talked about the 'Westminster bubble'. But this cosy consensus was thrown into confusion first by the election of Jeremy Corbyn to the leadership of the Labour Party, then by the Brexit referendum and finally by the campaign spearheaded by Boris Johnson (and his senior adviser, Dominic Cummings) to undermine the BBC.

Taking Corbyn seriously?

I experienced this bias to the centre ground in my years as a broadcast journalist based at Westminster. I was always acutely aware of how differently 'we' treated those on the fringes, and even outside the fringes, of the two main parties. Jeremy Corbyn was a case in point. As a backbencher he was never seen as a 'player', rarely invited to take part in discussions nor seen drinking with journalists, Hence, when he received enough votes (just) to run for the Labour leadership it took many months for BBC political journalists to treat him as a serious contender or to examine the ideas he was promoting. This was recognised by Katy Searle, then head of BBC News at Westminster, who told a Radio 4 audience: "Traditionally our focus here at BBC Westminster has been across the road. Jeremy's leadership has made us look beyond that."

Similarly, in the years prior to the EU referendum, Tory Eurosceptics were also regarded as somewhat beyond the pale. When Prime Minister John Major suggested that some of his own MPs were "one apple short of a picnic" (not in full possession of all of their faculties), he was doing no more than reflecting the Westminster consensus – which no doubt goes some way to explain why, through the referendum campaign and beyond, supporters of the Leave campaign have seen the BBC as fundamentally opposed to their view.

Human traffic: BBC–Tory Party

The second form of bias that affects the BBC results from the social make-up of the corporation and its staff. Conservative commentators are always quick to assert that BBC newsrooms are stuffed to the gunnels with middle class 'Guardian-reading pinkoes'. Even if that is the case it is undeniable that the BBC's political coverage has, for the last ten years, been dominated by Andrew Neil, a fine interviewer but also a man who chairs the board of the Tory-supporting magazine The Spectator and who, in his social media postings, makes no secret of his own right-wing leanings. In addition, in recent times there has been significantly more 'employment traffic' between senior BBC journalists and the Conservative Party than has taken place with Labour – to name but three examples: the chief media advisors to David Cameron, Theresa May and Boris Johnson (when Mayor of London) all formerly held senior posts at the BBC.

Nonetheless, the belief remains firmly fixed with many on the Right of politics that the BBC is biased to the Left. One noticeable effect of this allegation is a tendency for left-of-centre journalists at the BBC to bend over backwards in an attempt to be seen to be fair. During the 2019 general election campaign, for example, this took the form of broadcasting an excessive number of vox pops from areas that voted strongly to leave the EU. This was presumably because noisy denunciations of May's Government along the lines of, "Why don't they just get on with it?" made for far more lively radio or television than an anodyne "It's all very complicated" which was the not uncommon vox pop response from Remainers. No formal monitoring of the balance between vox pops from

Leave and Remain areas has been published to date; anecdotally, most observers would agree that the latter far outweighed the former. Speaking at a conference after the election, the BBC's chief political advisor, Richard Bailey, said that at some point during the election he had had to caution BBC journalists only to use vox pops if they were absolutely fundamental to the story. Commenting on the corporation's coverage of the EU referendum, a BBC correspondent told me how he was urged to actively seek out Leave stories that could lead the bulletins because Remain already had too many in that position.

The BBC 'selfish gene'

The third form of bias is much more deep-seated and results from the BBC's 'selfish gene' – its necessity as an organisation to survive and prosper. Since the awarding of the first BBC charter almost 100 years ago the notion of a public corporation dependent on a licence fee, operating under a Royal Charter granted by Parliament, dominating the broadcasting airwaves, has become increasingly contentious. Those broadly on the centre ground, and the Left, have always been happy with the dominant position of the BBC in the broadcasting landscape (at least that was the case) but for those on the Right the corporation has long been something to tolerate rather than celebrate. How this has played out inside the BBC, at an almost imperceptible level, is that rows with the Labour Party are regarded as unfortunate but not serious, whilst rows with the Conservative Party are both unfortunate and represent a potentially existential danger, a fear that has been more than validated recently by the actions and pronouncements of the Johnson Government.

The end game?

Whether the shrinking of the BBC to a fraction of its present size and output remains more than just a very thinly veiled threat remains to be seen, but as a threat it represents a very serious inhibitor of the BBC's ability to continue to pursue the quality journalism that has been its hallmark. In the current climate it's important that its critics accept that whatever their complaints of bias, and no matter how seemingly justified, BBC journalists are not motivated by either mendacity nor political prejudice but any perceived bias in the corporation's output results from the deep-seated institutional forces described above. These forces might have created a belief in some that the BBC **is** politically biased but in my view they are wrong. BBC journalism has its faults, it is certainly over-defensive and reluctant to admit mistakes, but these faults can be remedied. If the BBC is virtually destroyed then that can never be remedied and we will all be the poorer for it.

About the contributor

Ivor Gaber, now Professor of Political Journalism at the University of Sussex, has been involved in the coverage of politics for BBC TV and Radio, ITV News, Channel Four and Sky News.

Chapter 13

When Fake News is Growing, Why Kill a Truth-Teller?

Neither commercially nor state-driven, the BBC has long made a massive contribution to the ecology of UK broadcasting. Andrew Graham, the former Master of Balliol, reports on 'big data' research and shows that with a proliferation of echo chambers and the amplification of fake news, the BBC as a universally available 'truth-teller' is ever more required

The Government is gunning for the BBC. Overtly, the argument is that the BBC has over-reached itself and that current technology makes a publicly funded BBC redundant – at best a subscription based model will suffice. Covertly, Dominic Cummings regards the BBC as a left wing propagandist and has long argued that the priority of the Right should be to undermine the BBC's credibility. [1]

Let's start with the Cummings view. No independent review supports his claim; the BBC has been criticised by left as well as right; and BBC/Government tensions are nothing new. Above all, when facts conflict with political claims, the BBC must say so. Cummings' position is nothing more than the powerful wanting to be unquestioned and unaccountable. There could hardly be a better reason to *retain* the BBC.

The technology based criticisms of the BBC, with their intuitive appeal, are less easily dismissed. When multi-channel TV replaced monopoly, it seemed obvious that consumer choice should apply to broadcasting as with other goods and services. Similarly, in the era of the smart phone, to insist on retaining a public service broadcaster can easily appear anachronistic.

Multiple fallacies

Both arguments are mistaken. As argued elsewhere, [e.g. Graham and Davies, 1990 &1997, Graham, 1998, 2005 & 2013], the market view displays multiple fallacies. First, it confuses an "is" with an "ought" - that broadcasts can be sold does not automatically mean it is desirable that they should be. Second, its underlying economics is mistaken. Broadcasts are quasi-public goods (more like providing street lighting or National Parks than making a car); [2] they exhibit externalities; [3] and they have the potential to be "merit goods". [4]

More fundamentally, even within today's multi-channel world and even given the excellence of other providers, the broad reach of a BBC, funded by a licence fee, still fulfils a wider social role. It is not a fee to watch any particular programme, but to maintain the system as a whole and so increase the benefit for us all. The BBC has the potential to 'reach the parts that others do not' and by ensuring the quality of UK broadcasting *across the board* far from diminishing choice it adds to it. A subscription model, necessarily restricted to those who can pay and providing programming only for what viewers *already know they like* is a diminishing experience for them and for us all.

The smart phone, social media, and 'Big Data' research

Recent 'big data' research offers an equally critical take on whether the world of smart phones is really so perfect. First, it turns out that we are not the independent well-informed 'free choice' agents that mainstream economics assumes (and on which the model of consumer sovereignty is built). Rather we are all too often 'copiers', relying more on others whom we trust, than on our independent judgements. [5]

Furthermore, the bigger the group and the easier it is to find soulmates, the more we insulate ourselves from differing points of view and live in echo chambers [6] - precisely the world of the internet and social media. [7] Such echo chambers are perfect breeding grounds for fake news. Facts that run counter to the received view get denigrated as 'fake' while supportive information (both false and true) spreads like a virus. In two years the number of countries in which fake news is prevalent increased from 28 to 70. [8] Across the globe, nearly nine out of every ten people acknowledge having been duped at least once by fake news [9] - a proportion that would be even higher if it included those so duped they have still not realised it.

At the same time we have the fracturing of politics: from pro/anti Brexit in the UK, to pro/anti-Trump in the USA, to pro/anti Modi in India, the picture is the same. Such fracturing is undoubtedly partly driven by material factors, including globalisation and rising inequalities. But the growth of echo chambers and their boost to fake news can only amplify such fracturing – with all the damage to democratic discussion that this implies.

Given all this, contrast two approaches to the structure of the media: private sector media companies selling their wares in the market, free to push their own interests, including, if they so wish, political propaganda – versus a BBC with a public service commitment that is universally available, and still combined, as now, with private channels.

It seems inarguable that the first will intensify echo chambers, amplify fake news and increase the fracturing of the UK. The second, with its commitment to accuracy and its universal reach is one significant way to resist such fracturing.

And remember, who are these private channels? Pre-internet, broadcasting was, by far, the main supplier of news and images of society. Today, the supply of news, entertainment, and information is dominated by just four huge players: Facebook, Amazon, Apple and Microsoft.[10] All are private, US owned, pay little UK tax, and plagued by major breaches of data security. Two – Facebook and Amazon – show blatant disregard either for ethical concerns or employment practices. In such circumstances, we need a licence-funded, ethically committed, BBC like never before.

What next?

The BBC is far from flawless. Recent scandals around equal pay, lapses in programming standards, antagonistic interview styles – none help the BBC cause. With competition from Netflix and the loss of major sports events to broadcasters with deeper pockets, it also faces massive challenges. But, today, more than ever, the BBC is needed.

To re-establish itself, the BBC must reassert two fundamental reasons for its existence. First, in the words of Bernard Williams [2002], its primary goal must be - and be seen to be - that of a "truth-teller". In today's postmodernist world, there is, of course, no such thing as 'the truth', but there is still evidence – without that, news cannot, by definition, be fake! The BBC's priority must, therefore, be to promote those attempting to give authentic accounts of the world and to call out the quacks and the charlatans.

This requires renewed thought about how to achieve impartiality. It is no longer sufficient, if it ever was, simply to give equal air time to people on either side of a debate. As the Federation of American Scientists says about COVID-19: "Not all information is created equal. Some comes from professionals, who have years of experience in epidemiology. Some comes from unreliable anonymous internet accounts, bad actors, and hoaxers."[11]

Precisely!

Second, in the fragmented world of social media and echo chambers, the BBC must be the place where the UK comes together. It must, above all, be universally available, not restricted just to those able and willing to pay a subscription, and it must provide for all. In the world of the 2020s, the case for the BBC including hugely popular programmes, such as Strictly or Antiques Roadshow, as well as drama and documentaries, that pull in diverse groups of watchers goes up not down.

Finally, post-Brexit, our influence in the world relies primarily on our 'soft power' and the BBC remains at the very centre of such power. It is widely respected and watched across the globe. Moreover, it is rightly seen as a critical contributor to the success of the UK's creative industries. On these grounds alone, the case for its continuation is compelling.

Jettisoning Democracy

In a media world dominated by US giants, shot through with echo chambers and political fracturing breeding fake news, the BBC is needed more than ever. We need to pay the licence fee not just to watch any particular programme, but as a contribution by each of us to the public good that public service broadcasting can alone deliver. To give in to party political pressure that wishes to scrap the BBC – and for no other reason than to escape being accountable – would be to throw away a core part of our democracy.

About the contributor

Dr Andrew Graham is executive chair of the Europaeum (where he initiated a new scholarship across 17 leading European universities), founder and senior fellow of the Oxford Internet Institute and a trustee of Reprieve. Previous positions include Master of Balliol College, Oxford, non-executive director of Channel 4 Television, director of the Scott Trust, acting warden of Rhodes House, Rhodes trustee, fellow and tutor in Economics at Balliol, and economic adviser to the Rt Hon John Smith (Leader of the Opposition) and Prime Minister Harold Wilson.

Bibliography

CIGI-Ipsos (2019) https://www.cigionline.org/internet-survey-2019?gclid=EAIaIQobChMI-bGN2vzT5wIVyLTtCh1gAQc3EAAYASAAEgJyyPD_BwE (accessed 17/02/2020)

Federation of American Scientists (2020) Coronavirus Project https://fas.org/ncov/?utm_source=FAS+General&utm_campaign=fce70570c4-EMAIL_CAMPAIGN_2019_12_12_02_16_COPY_01&utm_medium=email&utm_term=0_56a7496199-fce70570c4-199334369#1581534080787-1893525f-dbef (accessed 17/02/2020)

Graham, A. and G. Davies (1990) *Why Private Choice Needs Public Broadcasting* Royal Television Society, London

Graham, A. and G. Davies (1997) *Broadcasting, Society and Policy in the Multimedia Age* John Libbey Media

Graham, A. (1998) "Broadcasting Policy and the Digital Revolution" in Jean Seaton (ed.) *Politics and the Media: Harlots and Prerogatives at the Turn of the Millenium* Blackwell Publishers

Graham, A. (2005) "It's the Ecology, Stupid" in Dieter Helm (ed.) *Can the Market Deliver: Funding Public Service Television in the Digital Age* John Libbey Publishing

Graham, A. (2013) "Is there still a place for Public Service Television?" in Robert G Picard and Paolo Sicialani (eds.) *Effects of the Changing Economics of Broadcasting* Reuters Institute for Journalism and the BBC Trust

Oxford Internet Institute (2019) The Global Disinformation Order, 2019, Global Inventory of Organised Social Media Manipulation https://comprop.oii.ox.ac.uk/wp-content/uploads/sites/93/2019/09/CyberTroop-Report19.pdf

Pentland, A. (2014) *Social Physics: How Good Ideas Spread-The Lessons from a New Science* Penguin Press

Syed, M. (2019) *Rebel Ideas: The Power of Diverse Thinking* John Murray Press

Williams, B. (2002) *Truth and Truthfulness: An Essay in Genealogy* Princeton University Press

References

1. A report of Cummings' blogs since 2004 was published in The Guardian, 21 January, 2020
2. One person's use does not compete with another and so, just as with the park, society's welfare is maximised by setting the price at zero.
3. Effects that are not captured in the market price, such as pollution from a factory. Examples in broadcasting are programmes that show excessive violence.
4. These are goods or services which consumers only realise *after* they have experienced them that they value them much more than they expected in advance. Education is an example. So, too, are programmes which are mind or experience expanding. By the same token, programmes that are literally mind numbingly repetitive would be 'demerit' goods. A private broadcaster, only interested in what you will pay now, will make too many demerit programmes and too few merit programmes.

5. See Pentland 2014
6. See Pentland 2014 and Syed 2019
7. A cautionary remark is needed. Research into the interaction between social media and echo chambers is in its infancy and diverse news sources may well reduce echo chambers. However, this possibility only increases the case for the BBC
8. According to the Oxford Internet Institute the spreading of fake news and toxic narratives has become the dysfunctional new 'normal' for political actors across the globe, thanks to social media's global reach (OII, 2019).
9. GIGI-Ipsos (2019)
10. Netflix is also a major competitor to BBC drama, but is not equivalent to the others across the pitch.
11. Federation of American Scientists, 2020.

Chapter 14

Does Boris Johnson have a Willie Whitelaw?

After decades of relatively benign acceptance, the BBC faces its most hostile political environment for a generation. Its contribution to British public life has never been more important, says Steven Barnett, but it needs a powerful friend in high places

It has been 40 years since the BBC faced a genuinely existential threat. There have been crises, battles, cuts, sackings and dramatic resignations in that time, but not since the election of Margaret Thatcher in May 1979 has the future of the BBC been seriously threatened by a powerful and deeply hostile government with a massive majority intent on doing it serious damage. This matters because the BBC matters: however much its enemies might love to portray it as an ageing, bureaucratic dinosaur from a bygone age, its contribution to the UK's creative, cultural and journalistic welfare is immense – not to mention its worldwide reputation as a source of trustworthy information in an age of fake news, and its vital role as a source of Britain's soft power in the post-Brexit era.

A benign political environment...

Lest we forget our political history, it's worth reminding ourselves quite how benign the political environment has been since Mrs Thatcher was seen off in 1990. Almost immediately after his accession to Downing Street, John Major demonstrated that he would not be playing to the vociferous anti-BBC right-wing gallery. In the wake of Britain's invasion of Kuwait in January 1991, Major was asked by his colleague Patrick Nicholls in the House of Commons to condemn the BBC for instructing reporters to say "British troops" rather than "our troops". It was a deliberate echo of the denunciation famously made by Margaret Thatcher during the 1982 Falklands War, inviting an equally censorious response. Nicholls and his baying cohorts would have been deeply disappointed by the response: "I believe", said Major, "that what the BBC is doing, in what has already been some remarkable reporting, is trying to keep proper balance."

When Blair followed Major in 1997, his new Culture Secretary Chris Smith was quick to acknowledge the BBC's importance as a unique British institution, and was instrumental in ensuring that it had the resources and the remit to lead Britain's digital evolution. Smith's successor, the late Tessa Jowell, was equally well disposed as she steered through the 2006 BBC charter. In 2010, the instinctive desire of an incoming Conservative PM to downsize BBC funding – using post-crash austerity measures as a convenient excuse – was constrained by his Liberal Democrat coalition partners. It was only following his unexpected though narrow 2015 election victory that David Cameron let loose his BBC sceptical wing and installed John Whittingdale as culture secretary to oversee the next BBC Charter. Even then, while succeeding to some extent in devising a framework for a more constrained BBC operation as well as imposing severe and wholly unnecessary financial cuts, Conservative moderates at least won the battle to keep a BBC of scope and scale.

... followed by visceral hostility

Then came the Johnson landslide: an opportunist PM who hates the BBC supported (some say controlled) by a chief adviser in Dominic Cummings who believes the BBC to be the Conservative Party's "mortal enemy", following an election in which Tory moderates were marginalised and the party faithful were more convinced than ever that BBC coverage was biased (an allegation which, of course, had Corbyn supporters laughing uproariously).

Even before the Downing Street boxes were unpacked, Johnson was announcing a "consultation" on whether non-payment of the BBC licence fee should remain a criminal offence – despite a comprehensive, independent review ordered by David Cameron and published less than five years ago concluding that the current arrangements were fair and proportionate.[1] Ministerial protestations that this was all about protecting the poor and vulnerable were somewhat undermined by the vocal support of serial BBC bashers from the Tory right whose altruistic concern for the disadvantaged had previously gone unnoticed.

This was the first shot by a government which knew well that decriminalisation would cost the BBC well in excess of £200 million while actually making life more difficult for poorer households which would simply be pursued with higher fines through the civil courts. That a full frontal assault was being planned gained even more credence by an apparently well-informed *Sunday Times* splash quoting a "senior source" saying that there would be a consultation on replacing the licence fee with a subscription model, that the BBC should be reduced to a few TV stations, a couple of radio stations and massively curtailed online presence, and that "the PM is firmly of the view that there needs to be serious reform. He is really strident on this."[2] That the source was almost certainly Cummings himself made the threat even more real.

BBC's absent friends...

All the comparisons with the equally hostile arrival of Margaret Thatcher 40 years ago are there – except one. At Thatcher's side, as Home Secretary as well as political confidant and loyalist, was her former opponent for the party leadership, Willie Whitelaw. Whitelaw was a moderate and a moderating influence on Thatcher's natural antagonism towards the BBC, and his guidance was acknowledged later in her premiership when she said – apparently in all innocence – "every Prime Minister needs a Willie". The abiding question for 2020 is – does Boris Johnson have a Willie?

Early signs are not good. Apart from a centralised Downing Street operation dominated by Cummings which will allow little discretion even for determined ministers, the new Culture Secretary Oliver Dowden is not a known BBC enthusiast. Moreover, newly installed as a minister in Dowden's department is none other than John Whittingdale, an appointment guaranteed to fuel speculation that the PM does indeed mean business. At the same time the Digital, Culture, Media and Sport Select Committee, which under its former chair Damian Collins could at least be expected to give the BBC a fair hearing, saw Collins replaced by Julian Knight who immediately declared that one of his first priorities was "to start an open conversation about how the BBC can be funded".[3]

Meanwhile, opposition parties who might in previous years have put up determined resistance feel bloodied and bruised by an election campaign which – in their view – gave the Conservatives in general and Johnson in particular an easy ride. While obvious signs of bias were difficult to discern – though some injudicious tweeting of Cummings' anonymous briefings by political editor Laura Kuenssberg fanned the flames of partisan anger – Labour, SNP and the Liberal Democrats all emerged deeply dissatisfied with BBC news coverage and are not immediately inclined to man the barricades in its defence.

... and powerful enemies

This resentment will be easy to exploit by a government focused on driving through an agenda of marginalisation. It will of course be assisted, as it has been for years, by powerful newspaper publishers which shamelessly exploit their online and off-line platforms to attack the BBC relentlessly for their own ideological and commercial reasons.

While the right-wing bias of Britain's national press has never been in doubt, analysis of the 2019 election coverage by Loughborough University demonstrated how shockingly skewed it has now become: weighted by circulation, the Labour Party's coverage towards the end was over 10 times more negative than the Conservative Party.[4] While some of these papers have historically had a paternalistic affection for the BBC, that has long been overtaken by a hard-nosed commercial opposition to a well-respected and trusted institution whose reputation for accurate and impartial news online makes it far more difficult for press operations to establish profitable online paywalls. Regardless of the clear democratic and societal benefits of a freely accessible and trusted disseminator of news and information, those publishers' leader writers and columnists routinely hurl abuse at the BBC and its licence fee.

Chief amongst the antagonists, of course, is Rupert Murdoch whose four national newspapers have frequently served as propaganda merchants for his publishing empire, never missing an opportunity to assail their readers with stories of BBC waste, bureaucracy, hypocrisy, incompetence or editorial bias. We can now expect this self-serving antagonism to increase in intensity, given that Murdoch's News UK is aggressively entering the radio market. Not only is TalkSPORT desperate to take over some of BBC 5 Live's exclusive rights to radio sports commentaries, but News UK has now announced that it will be launching Times Radio later this year to compete directly with BBC Radio 4. With BBC salaries under very close scrutiny, not least by the very newspapers determined to undermine it, the Murdoch-owned stations are set to benefit from any squeeze on BBC revenues. It may be naked commercialism, and the public interest may have disappeared in a corporate land grab, but the narrative will suit a government determined to inflict real and permanent damage on a public institution.

Netflix and die?

That narrative is reinforced through constant reference to the subscription streaming services which are gradually eating into viewing habits, particularly of the under 30s. How can we justify a compulsory £13 a month tax for the BBC, goes the contemporary argument, when Netflix is charging just £7.99 for all those amazing dramas and documentaries? The answer, of course, is that Netflix doesn't provide a trusted news, information and analysis service across all platforms, doesn't have a dedicated children's channel with home-produced children's programmes, doesn't provide a network of national and local radio stations, doesn't run an online operation admired throughout the world, doesn't promote new British musical talent, isn't universally available over the air, doesn't invest £2.7 billion per year in original UK content, and – crucially – doesn't make British programmes for British viewers throughout the nations and regions.

All this – and more – was outlined in last year's report by the House of Lords Select Committee on Communications whose title appropriately was *Public service broadcasting: as vital as ever.*[5] Given that Netflix is yet to return a penny profit, that more entertainment behemoths are bringing their own subscription offerings to market, and that the future of commercial streaming services are very uncertain, that report title is even more relevant to the BBC. In an age of economic and democratic uncertainty, it is as vital as ever.

This is not an argument for stasis, and a changing audiovisual environment demands a rational exploration of options. The licence fee should not be set in stone after the end of the current charter, and there is plenty of time for a sensible non-prejudicial review of alternative funding models that would preserve the BBC's unique qualities of universality, trust, authority and venture capital for the UK's creative economy (as Tessa Jowell famously called the licence fee); many countries, for example, are now switching to a household tax. A government serious about the public interest would at least investigate one of the most persuasive recommendations from that Lords report: establishment of an independent BBC Funding Commission to set the BBC licence fee in a transparent, non-partisan manner whose remit might be expanded to exploring other workable funding models.

At the moment, however, the BBC's future remains in the hands of a powerful, single-minded and apparently vengeful government intent on putting party before public service. Of course, the new consultation initiative, the damaging headlines and the new appointments may all be one gigantic bluff – no more than a Cummings-inspired plan to intimidate the BBC hierarchy and ensure that BBC news coverage is, if not exactly friendly, at least not overly critical. Either way, the future is unhealthy for the country and more dangerous than ever for the BBC which needs to galvanise its supporter base, whilst also seeking out sympathetic supporters in government. Despite Johnson's extra-marital exploits and unknown progeny – both less well documented than one might expect from a free press – BBC supporters must hope that our prime minister finds his Willie soon.

About the contributor

Steven Barnett is Professor of Communications at the University of Westminster and an established writer, author and commentator, who specialises in communications policy and regulation. Over the last 35 years, he has advised ministers and shadow ministers across the political spectrum, has given evidence to parliamentary committees and has served several times as specialist adviser to the House of Lords Communications Committee. He has directed numerous research projects on the structure, funding, and regulation of the media. He is on the editorial and management boards of British Journalism Review, and was for many years an Observer columnist. Books include The Rise and Fall of Television Journalism (Bloomsbury, 2011) and Media Power and Plurality (with Judith Townend, eds, Palgrave, 2015).Twitter: @stevenjbarnett.

References

1. TV Licence Fee Enforcement Review, July 2015, DCMS.
    https://www.gov.uk/government/news/independent-review-on-tv-licence-enforcement-published
2. https://www.theguardian.com/media/2020/feb/16/no-10-launches-attack-on-bbc-as-licence-fee-comes-under-threat
3. https://www.parliament.uk/business/committees/committees-a-z/commons-select/digital-culture-media-and-sport-committee/news/election-new-chair-dcms-committee-2019/
4. David Deacon et al, General Election 2019, Loughborough University.
    https://www.lboro.ac.uk/news-events/general-election/report-5/: figure 2.2
5. *Public service broadcasting: as vital as ever,* House of Lords Select Committee on Communications and Digital, November 2019.
    https://publications.parliament.uk/pa/ld201919/ldselect/ldcomuni/16/16.pdf

Chapter 15

Auntie on the Sports Journalism Dance Floor

The corporation's quest to secure a younger audience is captured most vividly in BBC Sport, says Tom Bradshaw, where something of an identity crisis is being publicly played out

It is no secret that the BBC, in common with other legacy media outlets, is in desperate pursuit of the young demographic. That pursuit of the under-35s is arguably at its most intense in sport. Sport is a gateway. If you attract and retain a young audience to sport, then you just might convert them to other content, too. Fail to attract and keep that young audience and, well, the audience projection charts don't look great, do they? Perilous, in fact.

These are disorientating times for sports journalism as social media continues to challenge and subvert the old rhythms and the old certainties. And like a fell-runner on new terrain, BBC Sport is in a process of trying to orientate itself in this uncertain digital habitat of Twitter storms and Instagram Stories. The teenagers and 20-something digital natives who have grown up on a diet of YouTube football press conferences, LADbible viral gaffes, and Twitter disputation over which players their club should sell or sign, are difficult for the BBC to reach. Young sports fans – football-lovers in particular – are used to a terrain of bumpily frantic transfer speculation and hollering reaction, while the BBC, traditionally at least, moves at a steadier pace and speaks in a more sober tone. *Match of the Day* retains a following of more than seven million over the course of the weekend – it has a form of cult status that shows how legacy, linear TV can still work – but BBC Sport requires reinvention if it is to be reinvigorated. Or does it?

"Two different audiences"

In its fight for enduring relevance and appeal, BBC Sport is manifesting symptoms of an identity crisis. One of the consequences of the digital revolution is that BBC Sport is now having to speak in at least two registers – or address two different audience segments – simultaneously. There is its more traditional, 'mature' audience which is used to a flow of BBC sports content that embodies the corporation's long-established values of impartial, steady – some might say 'straight-laced' – coverage. This audience still expects those values and the register they require to be upheld. Then there is the younger audience, which the BBC is desperate to tap into more deeply: an audience that hungers for, and expects, a more informal, 'fun' menu of content. To this second audience, the diet of content enjoyed by the first can be stuffily indigestible. To the first audience, the diet of content enjoyed by the second is trivial, light-weight, and perhaps 'un-BBC'.

"It's almost like two different audiences sometimes," is how one BBC staffer put it to me during an interview for an academic paper. She illustrated the dichotomy by describing how BBC Sport might simultaneously produce a serious, weighty story about the governance of the Qatar World Cup, and a piece about a man dressing up as a fridge to be a football club's mascot. While the latter is aimed at a younger audience, there is a wariness of trying too hard – appearing too desperate – to catch the eye of the young:

> We're trying to have fun stories but not write them like we're teenagers. We still want to write them in a solid BBC way but try and get them to different audiences... We have obviously a core audience but you don't want to be the dad at the disco. That's how we always say it – you don't want to be a 40-year-old man talking the language of a teenager because it just doesn't work. And I think sometimes that's what people think we're guilty of – just trying to be young and hip, and that's not what we're trying to do. We're just trying to engage with a different audience away from our core audience and I think people do struggle with that sometimes.

Although the 'Dad at the Disco' phenomenon is one that Auntie is keen to avoid, some of the moves from BBC Sport suggest it is keen to meet its young audience half way on the sports journalism dance floor. "A couple of years ago our journalism at the BBC was pretty straight-laced," another staffer for BBC Sport tells me, but now "social media and the way that things are presented can sometimes change the way you might approach a story. Rather than telling the story in a traditional paragraph-by-paragraph way, social media sometimes means we tell the story in a way that's a bit lighter."

This sounds innocuous enough, even sensible. Isn't sport all about lightness, anyway? Groin strains, niggling dressing room spats, and all that? But the serious consequences of the belief in lightness are now being played out, not least as BBC Sport thinks about how it can reduce its spending given the inevitable budgetary challenges that lie ahead.

Star sacrifices

Upon the altar of enduring relevance, BBC Sport appears to be offering big-beast sacrifices, particularly in the field of radio. There has been a bonfire of the 'pale, male and stale' at Radio 5 Live as the station has rapidly parted company with a list of successful, long-serving, nationally regarded broadcasters. First to go was John Inverdale, who took off his BBC radio headset for good following the 2019 Cheltenham Festival. Since then other world-class sports broadcasters have followed, including horse racing correspondent Cornelius Lysaght and presenter Mark Pougatch. Hit a certain age and command a certain pay packet at BBC Sport and it seems you have some very good reasons to be looking over your shoulder.

Broadcasters of a certain vintage at other outlets have raised their concerns in ways that BBC insiders, for obvious reasons, are reluctant to. Clive Tyldesley, the football commentator, has spoken out against what he terms "reflex ageism" while Jeff Stelling, the presenter of Sky Sports' 'Soccer Saturday', tweeted: "So @markpougatch not presenting on 5 live any more. Sad that his total professionalism will be replaced by someone who is considered to be more in touch with the youth of today, even if they know sod all about football or interviewing. He can't say it so I will" (9 January 2019). The assumption behind much of this is that BBC Sport is aggressively pursuing the development of a more diverse workforce – a workforce that it believes is more likely to resonate with a younger audience – but that in so doing it is jettisoning high-calibre journalists.

Noble intentions, ignoble journalism?

Diversity, properly understood and applied, can be editorially invigorating. Multiple backgrounds and multiple perspectives can ensure a mind-expanding breadth of coverage for audiences. Diversity can be the oxygen for variety, the stimulant for insight. This applies on sports desks just as much as it does on news desks. As I argue in my recent book *Sports Journalism: The State of Play* (Routledge, 2020) sports journalism has not always been at the vanguard on the long march to equality, but the landscape is changing and sport – and the way it is mediated – is a potent weapon in changing social attitudes. However, we are on perilous ground editorially if the pursuit of a diverse workforce becomes a mission in which experience, insight and journalistic skill are cast aside. Noble journalism can become a casualty of noble intentions. Diversity is vital and still needs its champions, of which I am one, but it must not be allowed to become a term that is unthinkingly invoked to justify purges and ill-conceived editorial plans.

Game-changing decisions at BBC Sport

During the spring and summer of 2019, the BBC ran a campaign called Change the Game which highlighted the amount of elite women's sport taking place across the summer as well as its own coverage of it. The target demographic was clear, with the corporation working with rapper Ms Banks to create an anthem for the campaign that, according to a BBC press release, "aims to empower and inspire the next generation of women who might follow in these athletes' footsteps". Moreover, the coverage of the summer's action – of football, cricket, netball and tennis – was just the beginning, said the BBC's director of sport, Barbara Slater. Much of the content was excellent, and the coverage of the football World Cup in particular ensured women's sport acquired a new audience, a fact which is to be celebrated. But while Slater says the ambition of BBC Sport's output has never been bigger, it seems the corporation thinks it can achieve these brave new ambitions without some of its best-established names. The pursuit of a young audience (the "next generation") seems to be equating to a steady whittling down of the older generation. Ms Banks or Cornelius Lysaght? BBC Sport seems to have nailed its colours to the mast.

Then there is the issue of funding. Is the current licence fee model actually inhibiting the BBC's ability to attract a sport-loving under-35 audience? The diminishing list of major sporting events that the BBC can afford to pay the live broadcast rights for has prompted the corporation to pursue niches – which is fantastic if you like basketball or touch rugby (and it is to be welcomed that minority sports are getting coverage on the BBC), but to pull in large young audiences the BBC arguably needs a few big signings. The licence fee is not adequate to make these deals; it cannot compete with the billions Sky and BT Sport put into football, and Amazon Prime's new subscription-based venture into the Premier League makes the BBC's use of a hypothecated tax to pay for sports coverage look out of step. One suggestion is that BBC Sport's live coverage could be hived off from its sports news, with the former funded by paid-for subscription and the latter by a reduced licence fee. By pulling in a younger audience to its live coverage, the BBC might then be able to direct that audience to its sports news coverage, too – and keep it.

There are flashes of depth and perceptiveness to BBC Sport's news output. Its editor, Dan Roan, has a background as a politics, finance and news reporter, and it shows. Roan generally brings a gravitas to the BBC's coverage of the big off-the-field stories, from doping to human rights. That depth can be what helps set BBC Sport apart from many other outlets. The fear is that such depth is being undermined by the headlong chase of the young demographic. And that, ultimately, is a disservice to everyone.

About the contributor

Tom Bradshaw is an academic and sports journalist. His latest book, *Sports Journalism: The State of Play*, with Daragh Minogue, is published by Routledge. He is a senior lecturer in the School of Media at the University of Gloucestershire, and has covered sport around the globe for a range of online and print titles. He contributes to BBC Radio's rugby output, while his academic research focuses on media ethics.

Chapter 16

The BBC in a political minefield

The crisis facing the corporation may be existential. Raymond Snoddy, the doyen of media writers, knows a 'BBC crisis' when he sees one. He looks at the tensions between the Government and the BBC following Boris Johnson's 2019 landslide victory

It was December 2019 and Boris Johnson was on the stump looking for a 'dead cat' to distract from some pretty bizarre behaviour in Grimsby. He had refused to look at a picture of a sick boy waiting for treatment on a Leeds hospital floor on a reporter's phone. Instead he had pocketed the phone. It had the makings of a major gaffe.

Nothing quite like it had ever happened before. As a gaffe it more than matched Prime Minister Gordon Brown's description in the 2010 election campaign of Labour supporter Gillian Duffy as a "bigoted woman", a remark accidently picked up by a microphone and one that led to an afternoon of grovelling apologies. In 2019, Johnson later apologised for taking the journalist's phone.

Enter the 'Dead Cat'

Bojo found his 'dead cat' at the next campaign stop: the BBC. An interesting afternoon around Sunderland led to the story moving on from the NHS and the effects of austerity to the future of the BBC, its funding and licence fee. BBC finances had not been an issue in the election campaign, which was dominated by the funding crisis facing the NHS and the main theme to 'Get Brexit done'.

Then an employee at Ferguson's haulage company, in what was then the Labour stronghold of Washington, Co. Durham, asked Johnson: "Why don't you abolish the TV licence, please?"

The Prime Minister, live on Sky News, asked: "For everybody?"

"Yes," replied the worker..

Johnson appeared slightly surprised before replying that he was not going to make such an unfunded commitment so late in the campaign.

"What I certainly think is that the BBC should cough up and pay for the licences for the over-75s as they promised to do. At this stage we are not planning to get rid of all TV licences, although I am certainly looking at it," Johnson said.

The Prime Minister noted he was under pressure "not to extemporise on the hoof" but added that you had to ask yourself whether that kind of approach to funding a media organisation made sense in the long term given the way other organisations managed to fund themselves.

"The system of funding by what is effectively a tax on everybody that has a TV, it bears reflection, let me put it that way. How long can you justify a system whereby everybody who has a TV has to pay for a particular segment of TV?" Johnson explained.

After the exchange it was revealed that the future of the TV licence was indeed under consideration in Downing Street and that the Prime Minister's main advisor, Dominic Cummings, was a long-term opponent of the licence fee. Number 10 admitted it was looking at the possibility of funding the BBC by voluntary subscription or at the very least de-criminalising non-payment of the licence, which was likely to have a similar effect.

The 'dead cat' did its job

Did the question come out of the blue, and was the carefully worded, thought out response to it coincidental? Perhaps, but at the very least Johnson may have spotted an opportunity. Certainly the attack on the BBC licence fee quickly dominated the headlines and running orders, turning the story of the four-year-old on the floor of a Leeds hospital into old news.

The BBC and the over-75s

What of Johnson's supposedly off-the-cuff remarks about the BBC covering free licence fees for the over-75s "as they had promised to do"? The BBC promised no such thing. When the then Chancellor George Osborne tried to force the BBC to take on the full obligation of the over-75s previously funded by government the Corporation warned privately that this would mean the closure of BBC 2, the BBC News Channel, all BBC local radio stations and the national radio services for Scotland, Wales and Northern Ireland. The Government backed down and the compromise agreement meant the transfer of responsibilities for the free licences would be phased in between 2016 and 2020.

In was a poisoned chalice. The BBC was explicitly given the freedom to decide what to do. It would face unpopularity, rather than the Government, if the corporation ended the concession.

Paying all of the free licences for the over 75s, many of whom are relatively well off, would cost the BBC around £750 million a year, a sum that would rise to £1 billion a year by the end of the decade because of an ageing population. Such a course, covering 20 per cent of the BBC's total budget, would inevitably mean significant cuts to BBC services.

After a public consultation Sir David Clementi, the BBC chairman, announced "a difficult but fair" decision to continue free licence fees for the over-75s who are on pension support but the rest would have to pay. Even that will cost the BBC £250 million a year, and possibly even more, if the licence fee issue encourages more over 75s to apply for pension support.

The decision to look again at decriminalising the licence fee and turn non-payment into a civil debt seems odd because Prime Minister Cameron set up an inquiry into the issue in 2015 and called in leading criminal barrister David Perry. The QC decided that "in the overall public interest" the current system should be maintained although he asked for more research on why a disproportionate number of women came before the courts. Perry noted that frequent claims that the system clogged up magistrates courts – still being repeated today – were untrue. Magistrates dealt with non-payment fines in batches and they accounted for only 0.3 per cent of court time. Perry also noted that de-criminalisation would inevitably lead to an increase in evasion, something that the BBC estimates could cost up to £200 million a year.

Whither the licence fee?

As for the licence fee, it is guaranteed under the BBC's current Royal Charter until 2027. There is a mid-term review in 2022, by coincidence the BBC's centenary year, although that is seen as an opportunity to look at the level of licence fee, currently £154.50 and rising with inflation.

Johnson might just go for a crowd pleaser and try to reduce the licence fee although that would be controversial. Even more controversial, and something that would lead to a legal challenge, would be any attempt by the Government to try use its strong majority to try to overturn the Royal Charter midway through its life and replace the licence fee with a subscription system.

Boris and the BBC – low-level war?

The structural problems that the BBC is facing – or could soon face – are only part of 'the Boris Johnson problem'. There are Conservative allegations of bias against the BBC both in the run-up to Brexit and from the 2019 general election campaign itself.

Considerable bitterness arose from the BBC's vigorous pursuit of a Boris Johnson interview with Andrew Neil. As the clock ticked down to the general election and there was no sign of Boris, at least as far as Neil was concerned, the forensic interviewer launched what amounted to an on-air attack on the Prime Minister.

Neil, once Johnson's boss when the future Prime Minister was editor of *The Spectator*, did not pull his punches. Such an interview, Neil told his audience, was a matter of trust.

"The theme running through our questions is trust, and why at so many times in his career in politics and journalism, critics and sometimes even those close to him have deemed him to be untrustworthy," Neil said on live television. He listed a number of Johnson's policy proposals and asked whether Johnson could be trusted to deliver on his promises.

Neil did not get his interview.

Boris and the BBC – more skirmishes

Non-appearance at crucial interviews was one thing but Johnson also banned all his ministers from appearing on Radio 4's flagship *Today* programme where they used to command the 8.10am main political slot but faced vigorous questioning.

Johnson did do what was seen as a "soft" interview with *BBC Breakfast's* Dan Walker.

Sarah Sands, editor of the *Today* programme, accused Downing Street of deploying 'Trumpian' tactics in banning ministers from appearing on the programme and accused the Government of using its majority to "put the foot on the windpipe of the BBC".

Is this the mother of all BBC/Government rows?

There have always been rows between the BBC and politicians of all parties but the depth and range of current animosity appears unprecedented.

The out-going director-general of the BBC, Tony Hall, rejected all claims of bias in the corporation's election coverage. "Criticism," he wrote in an article in *The Daily Telegraph.* "is to be expected as the national broadcaster... But the fact that criticism came from all sides of the political divide shows to me that we were doing our job without fear or favour."

Are the current attacks on the BBC just the normal cut and thrust of general election politics? After all, apart from ministers not turning up to the *Today* programme little of a concrete nature has actually happened.

The record going forward will answer that question but in the meantime it would be wise to assume that an unprecedented degree of malice is informing the Johnson government's attitude to the BBC and great damage could be the result.

If any of the gaffes, or his unwillingness to face serious questioning, had any effect on the electorate it was difficult to discern as Johnson won an 80-seat majority and pushed on with getting Brexit done. Will he 'do' the BBC next?

About the contributor

Raymond Snoddy is the former Media Editor of *The Times* and Media Correspondent of the *Financial Times*. He is now a freelance writer on media matters.

A longer version of this chapter will appear in BORIS, BREXIT AND THE MEDIA edited by John Mair, Tor Clark, Neil Fowler, Raymond Snoddy and Richard Tait (Abramis, Forthcoming)

Chapter 17

A Letter to the New DG

Fiona Chesterton pens a note to await the arrival of the new director general in the summer of 2020. She is pleased about the appointment of the first woman to the post but urges the new DG not to be diverted by gender issues. Instead, she calls on her to strike out boldly with a new plan for the BBC to take the battle for its funding direct to the audience

Fiona Chesterton,
Cambridge, England.

The Director-General,
New Broadcasting House,
London W1A 1AA.
(please forward to Salford Quays if necessary)

Dear ....

First of all, many congratulations. At last!

You don't know me, but I am one of the many women who helped in our various modest ways to blaze the trail: one that has led to your great achievement in becoming the first woman to take not just the top job at the BBC but arguably the most important position in the cultural life of our country. When I joined the BBC as a trainee journalist back in the mid-70s – when you were still in primary school – I was the only woman among eight recruits. When I started work in the TV newsroom soon after, certain genres of reporting, including politics and sport, were considered firmly male terrain. By the mid-80s when I had become a senior producer in Current Affairs, I was one of the first to negotiate successfully a return to work part-time after maternity leave. Another decade on, I was a commissioning editor, working with female channel controllers, executive producers and heads of department.

So we've come a long way – but I really don't want the way you carry out your role to be in any way defined by your gender. I hope *The Daily Mail* and *The Sun* don't feel the need to remind readers of your age, your marital status, the number of children you have, or what you wore to the Culture committee hearings in the House of Commons or to the BAFTAs. Maybe, though, they could mention your killer heels – but only if in reference to how you take on Government ministers and their supporters who seem set on taking down the BBC not just a peg or two but simply taking it down.

You surely have a fight on your hands.

I am looking to you to waste no time in getting on the front foot, maybe in running shoes rather than in heels. I hope you offered the appointment panel a clear vision of how the BBC can not only survive but thrive into its second century. I also hope that now you have got the job, you will be out on the TV, on radio, on social media and on platforms around the country to communicate that vision to the audience. Of course, you must take the BBC's staff and a whole range of institutional and industry stakeholders with you as well but it is the British public whose hearts and minds you must engage first and foremost. It is their trust and their love – yes, that is the right word, not a more commercial word like 'custom' – which must be won, or rather won back.

I don't have to tell you it won't be easy. The last few years, as we know, have not been good ones for the BBC. It's not just the technology diverting the audience and the streaming services, with their huge pockets, rapacious mindset, and (currently) modest subscriptions, but the largely self-inflicted wounds, especially around executive pay – where the adjective 'rapacious' also comes to mind – and the poor handling of some of the journalistic challenges, especially since the EU referendum. What is so tragic is that this has overshadowed what has been a generally rather fine period for its programmes, especially in drama.

The most wounding charge for the BBC to counter is surely that it has become part of the so-called metropolitan elite rather than a champion and a forum for the audience. The politicians now understand how that critique has wounded them – how they stopped listening let alone responding to the needs of their constituents, gliding above them in a sea of lobbyists, wealthy donors, and smart parties in the so-called Westminster bubble. Dare I suggest that there are some key lessons that some of the smarter politicians – and their advisers – have learnt and are beginning to put into action and which you might think about adopting too? Show your audience that you 'get it'.

I would suggest these might include:

1. Recognising how tough life is for the majority of your audience and that every pound that can be saved from the cost of living is worthwhile – hence the appeal of making the licence fee a voluntary payment. Understand that median household disposable income in 2019 in the U.K. was less than £30,000 per year, according to the Office of National Statistics An after-tax income of £100,000 a year, which would be considered as relatively modest in television circles, puts such people in the top 1 per cent of earners. Your pay as DG and the pay of the so-called top talent at the BBC is therefore off the scale. Think about that in the context of the debate about gender pay between woman and men on £250,000-plus per annum.

2. Diversity on and off screen is vital – but diversity of opinion and social background is as important as the current interpretation of this over-used word, mainly focussed as it is around ethnicity and gender. This is particularly important in the composition of your newsrooms. Realise that you might not share some of the tastes of your audience and they do not share yours. Hence why *Mrs. Brown's Boys* beat *Fleabag* in the recent National Television Awards. So don't keep mentioning *Fleabag,* brilliant as it was, almost as shorthand for programme excellence in every context.

3. Don't neglect your 'core' voters/audience, particularly in the pursuit of youth. Look at the demographics: while London and the other cities where you have your out-of-London offices are relatively young, at the last count there were nearly 12 million people, close to one-in-five of the population who are over 65, with a higher proportion in country areas and in towns, where a quarter, or even nearly a third, of the population may be old. The trend, of course, as ONS figures show, is for a further ageing of society.

So how would I suggest that you might show that you 'get it'?

By the time you read this letter, the Department for Digital, Culture, Media & Sport may have already moved after its consultation period to decriminalise the licence fee. Can I urge you not to fight this but to take the hit of £200m a year? It is not a good look to seem to want to retain the right to drag mainly poor women through the courts.

Secondly, make a bold commitment to freezing executive pay, including your own, for the next five years, with a concomitant commitment to freezing the level of the licence fee at, say, £156 a year, that is £3 a week.

Explain that the production arm of the BBC, BBC Studios, now operates commercially and must pay market rates for talent. Explain also that will mean that in the future some areas of the BBC, especially drama and entertainment, will require additional financial commitment beyond the licence fee, from global investment and additional customer subscription in the UK. A BBC Premiere channel and BBC Premiere Box Sets service could surely attract a few million subscribers at home, and even more beyond the UK as a supplement but not a replacement for the licence fee. Thin end of the wedge, do I hear you say? No, just a recognition that the BBC can no longer do what it has done for years, which is expand onto every new platform and pay for every sort of content out of the licence fee alone.

On diversity, you have to play a longer game to see results as you are talking about cultural change. However, you can make a start by a commitment to genuine devolution and diversification of commissioning powers throughout the UK. This would include a reversal of the recent decision by your News management to concentrate commissioning powers at the top of the organisation. It would also involve substantial investment in local journalism and in working with colleges, community organisations and independent producers to support young and new talent from every background.

As for the pursuit of 'yoof' (which to my certain knowledge the BBC has been pursuing for most of the past 40 years), I say, focus on what the BBC does best and don't patronise the young. The 'yoof' that the BBC were pursuing in the 80s, when Janet Street-Porter was brought in to target this elusive audience, are now middle-aged and probably stalwart fans of *Strictly*. Some of the toddlers who were transfixed daily by the adventures of the Teletubbies in the late 90s are now parents themselves, and pleased that CBeebies is still providing safe and trusted pre-school entertainment.

While I am thinking of children's TV, I do hope you will commit to the centrality of high-quality, UK-produced, programming for children as a core part of the BBC's offer to the audience. I wrote about that a few years ago at a time when the BBC was beginning to be on the defensive from the majority Cameron-Osborne Tory Government ('Who's Looking After the Children?' in *The BBC Today: Future Uncertain*). I see now that the then Secretary of State for Culture, Media and Sport, John Whittingdale, is back at his old department. One of the ideas he promoted before was using some of the licence fee to set up a separate contestable fund for children's producers. This was designed not to deal with a deficit at the BBC but at the commercial UK broadcasters, like ITV who had cut their commitment to children's TV in the previous few years. The Young Audience Content Fund was set up only last year, and so far has only made a very modest contribution to boosting production. I urge you to make the case for the BBC to continue to take the lead in this area – and that its investment and track record should not be lightly abandoned for an as-yet-unproven new model.

The BBC's heritage, its size and scale, its internationally-known brand is not something to be lightly abandoned either. Please fight with your heart as well as your mind to get the people who pay for it to fight for it too.

It's a good fight and one you can still win.

Good luck and best wishes,

Fiona Chesterton

About the contributor

Fiona Chesterton had a long career in public service broadcasting, working as a journalist, producer, news editor and commissioning editor at the BBC and Channel 4. In 2008 she was awarded a Fellowship of the Royal Television Society for outstanding contribution to the industry. In the past few years she has written on TV issues in books and online and is currently writing a book, part family history, part childhood memoir.

Chapter 18

Democracy – and not just the BBC – is in peril

If it is to survive the BBC will have to change enormously – again – but the Government has polluted the forums for debating its future, argues Simon Albury

1992: "The licence fee may become unsustainable"

In the 1990s there were three Directors of Public Affairs in ITV. David Cameron at Carlton, now an ex-prime minister, Chris Hopson at Granada, the cleverest and now chief executive NHS Providers, and me at United News & Media, now retired, unemployable and Chair of the Campaign for Broadcasting Equality CIO.

One person we all admired was Patricia Hodgson, then the BBC's lead propagandist, and in particular we very much admired what we called "the Hodgson book" – a clever, exemplary campaigning device. Hodgson had been secretary of the BBC and knew all its secrets. At this point she was head of the BBC's Policy and Planning Unit.

Hodson's preface said the reports in the book, titled *Paying for Broadcasting: The Handbook*[1], published 28 years ago in 1992, "contain much of the data needed to inform decisions about the future shape of broadcasting".

Many of the reports were tough to read but you didn't need to read them unless you wanted to challenge their assertions – as the book led with an executive summary. Clever! The whole point of the Hodgson book appeared to be a justification for a significant increase the in the licence fee which it said needed to be "uprated in a more generous way."

The book also carried a warning, "The BBC probably needs to maintain a market share of at least one-third. Below 25 to 30 per cent the licence fee may become unsustainable."

Less than a year after the book came out, Hodgson was promoted to the BBC board as director of policy. In 2000 she left to become chief executive of the Independent Television Commission. From 2006-2010, she returned to the BBC as a member of the BBC Trust. She joined the

Ofcom board in 2011 and served as chair from 2014-2018. Hodgson was made a CBE in1995 and a Dame in 2004.

Seldom seen on public platforms, Hodgson has wielded significant influence in the corridors of power. The BBC has enemies, Dame Patricia is not one of them. What she says has to be taken seriously. On 28 December 2019, Dame Patricia made a rare public appearance on the BBC Radio 4 *Today* programme. What she said was not a shock to me. I'd heard it from others with an interest in broadcasting policy, but that Dame Patricia said it in public was:

> *The licence fee is guaranteed until 2027, but in the age of Netflix and Spotify and YouTube, I think the BBC needs to work its way to a new funding model. If it's to survive.*

> *Now, I believe that it should and will survive. It's the foundation of our creative industries, our shared culture as a nation, but also because in post-Brexit Britain it will be very important globally, the world service particularly, and I think a model for change should start with the licence fee settlement in 2022.*

> *We should start to either freeze or reduce the license fee to incentivize the BBC into using broadband technology for subscription top-ups, so we're progressing to a new funding base after 2027.*

A well-placed friend told me: "It is clear Patricia believes change is speeding up and the simple licence fee won't sustain – just witness the annual decline now in under-35s' viewing of the schedule... almost 20 per cent this year."

At the end of the *Today* interview, Dame Patricia concluded: "The BBC has changed enormously, since Lord Reith's day. And if it's to survive, it will have to change enormously again." Hodgson's view was consistent with the warning she had promulgated on behalf of the BBC in 1992.

Rise of Cummings, Fall of Hall

Until Friday, 13 December 2019, the BBC had been its own worst enemy. It performs poorly on diversity and has wilfully published misleading data.[2] This is a view supported by Ofcom.[3] The BBC has been too slow to act on diversity and increasing regionalism. When it came to pay equality and personal service contracts, the director-general's own evidence to the Commons Digital, Culture, Media & Sport Select Committee revealed starkly that while Tony Hall may have had his hands on the levers of power, they had diminishing leverage lower down the organisation where senior managers could disregard the higher-level goals. Management wasn't delivering and it seemed Hall couldn't get a grip on it. On 24 October, Sharon White, the Ofcom chief executive, had to send an unprecedented letter of criticism of the BBC's performance to Tony Hall. The message was shape up or else.[4]

The BBC board clearly thought something needed to be done. In an act of masterly and smooth establishment engineering, the chairman, Sir David Clementi, must have offered Hall the revolver and said it didn't need to be used until a soft landing with status had been found. The soft landing turned out to be appointed chair of the National Gallery. All but one of the National Gallery directors are appointed by the Prime Minister but not the chair. Tony Hall was appointed a trustee of the National Gallery on 1 November 2019. The trustees made Hall chair three months later.

On that Friday, 13 December, the BBC found it had a worse enemy. Dominic Cummings had entered Downing Street with enormous power. Cummings is an enemy of the BBC and also of democratic checks and balances.

Ofcom – nobbled?

The Sunday Times reported (and others have confirmed privately) that No. 10 had "urged the regulator Ofcom to drop Dame Melanie Dawes as its next chief executive in favour of someone who would challenge the BBC". I'm very keen to see Ofcom continue to challenge the BBC but it was quite wrong for government to seek to block the CEO chosen by the Ofcom board on that basis.

In 2017, when Ofcom proposed to do an inadequate job on regulating the BBC on diversity, there was a political argy-bargy. Government ministers Matt Hancock and Karen Bradley gave Ofcom a good kicking and Ofcom produced better plans. A proper tension between government and regulator played out in public. That's how it is supposed to work. Ofcom is working on the latest public service broadcasting review. It could be important. The appointment of a different CEO, with the government's agenda, would devalue anything Ofcom says in its public service broadcasting Review.

Eventually, after months of government procrastination, Dame Melanie Dawes was appointed on 12 February 2020. It was also announced that the Ofcom chair, Lord Burns, would step down early.

A former Government advisor told me: "Terry has had to fall on his own sword to get Dawes appointed. From the government's point of view, better to choose the chairman rather than influence the choice of CEO. The Government have achieved what they wanted, in fact they've done better."

We must hope that the Government's basis for appointing the new chair will be their suitability for delivering Ofcom's long-term remit rather than their willingness to deliver the government's short-term-agenda. Ofcom should not be nobbled.

The Press - to be nobbled?

On 3 February, Downing Street excluded journalists it didn't like from a briefing and their more favoured colleagues marched out with them in support. In *The Daily Mail*, Stephen Glover, who says he shares many of Cummings' criticisms of the BBC, declared he was shocked. Under the headline "Denying journalists access to briefings is outrageous censorship that Boris Johnson should be ashamed of", Glover wrote:

> *Instead of putting itself under proper media scrutiny, No 10 is feuding with our main national service broadcaster – and now opening up another front against media organisations.*

> *All this comes from President Trump's playbook. In his case, he rails against newspapers such as the Washington Post and the New York Times while putting himself and members of his administration at the disposal of supportive channels such as Fox News.*

> *That is not how we do things in Britain. We have a tradition here, though Mr Cummings and Mr [Lee] Cain [Downing Street communications director] may not like it, of allowing a range of voices in the media, some of which are bound to be critical of the government of the day.*

> *I never thought I would live to see a Tory administration blackballing journalists and publications it dislikes.*

The Government hostility to the BBC and to democratic processes sets the wrong environment for a reasonable debate about the licence fee.

Commons DCMS Committee - nobbled?

Until 29 January 2020, Damian Collins served as chair of the Commons DCMS Committee for more than four years. I watched many of the sessions live and read much of the evidence taken. With one exception[5], Collins was calm, forensic, fair, and balanced.

In March 2019, the Houses of Commons Committee on Privileges held Dominic Cummings in contempt of parliament for failing to attend the Collins DCMS Committee. Damian Collins said: "The Dominic Cummings case highlights the need for parliament to define in law what its powers should be to require witnesses to attend hearings, and what sanctions should apply if they do not... The current powers have been tested to their limits and found wanting."[6] Some suggest that it was Cummings who ensured that Collins was not re-elected chair of the Commons DCMS Committee, although, while this has the smell of truth, I have not been able to source this adequately. It may not be true.

In his public pitch for the job, Julian Knight, the new chair of the committee, said he would lead what amounts to a MPs Royal Commission "into the future of the BBC, how it is funded, it's rules on impartiality, the way it interacts with the private sector - it often crushes it by using it's awesome spending power - and what role can it play in a world dominated by the likes of Netflix."[7] Sadly, Knight doesn't seem to be an impartial chairman, starting with an open mind.

Democracy undermined

Nevertheless, the idea of a far-reaching enquiry could provide a useful forum for exploring different options, not least from potential candidates for director-general, for the ways in which the BBC "will have to change enormously again."

On 9 February 2020, Adam Boulton published a column in *The Sunday Times* headlined "No. 10 is trying to control the media, and everyone in our democracy should be afraid".[9] Boulton wrote:

> *What is important is that readers, listeners, and viewers are increasingly missing out on the information they need to function as independent citizens in a democratic society. Instead they are being manipulated by elected governments anxious to avoid being held to account by any outside force, be it parliament, the judiciary or the media."*

And later:

> *Although the Johnson administration likes to be seen as radical and transformative, its behaviour continues a depressing trend to politicise the provision of official information which began in the New Labour years.*

The difference today is that the executive branch seems willing to do away with any of the traditional checks and balances to unfettered government including the free press.

By considering nobbling Ofcom, the press and the Commons DCMS Committee, the government has sought to pollute the forums in which a sensible debate on the future of the BBC could take place.

As Dame Patricia said:

The BBC has changed enormously, since Lord Reith's day. And if it's to survive, it will have to change enormously again.

It's the foundation of our creative industries, our shared culture as a nation, but also because in post-Brexit Britain it will be very important globally, the World Service particularly..."

The BBC is in peril not because it will have to change if it is to continue to deliver the attributes Hodgson spells out. The BBC is in peril because, as Adam Boulton diagnosed: "No. 10 is trying to control the media, and everyone in our democracy should be afraid."

Postscript

This chapter was completed before the Government reshuffle on 13 February 2020. The reshuffle has reinforced and accelerated the tendency to dispense with the normal checks and balances that deliver better government. As Robert Shrimsley observed in the *Financial Times*: "There is a counter-argument that this (losing the chancellor) and other moves in the reshuffle will increase the unity at the heart of the administration. All those still in place will have signed up to pull in the same direction. But good government often depends on senior ministers – and the chancellor in particular – being able to fight bad ideas. Mr Johnson's cabinet has just seen the price of defiance." [10]

About the contributor

Simon Albury writes in a personal capacity. He is chair of the Campaign for Broadcasting Equality CIO, a former chief executive of the Royal Televisions Society and was founder chair of the Centre for Investigative Journalism. He has worked for the BBC and ITV.

References

1.   Tim Congdon et al (1992), *Paying for Broadcasting*, London, Routledge

2. Simon Albury (20 August 2019) "Diversity: The BBC may fool itself but it won't fool the Lords" Open Democracy
3. Simon Albury (18 November 2019) "The BBC has failed on diversity: why were the Lords too timid to say so?" Open Democracy
4. Sharon White letter to Tony Hall (24 October 2019) Ofcom www.ofcom.org.uk
5. The exception was the hearing on 17th July 2019 at which the Committee explored the detail of the debate within the BBC at the time and how the decision was made to accept the Government's offer over-75s licence fees. The questioning led by Julian Knight and Philip Davies was unusually aggressive and appeared to be trying to pin something on the BBC that was not borne out by the facts.
6. Digital, Culture, Media and Sport Committee. Oral evidence: BBC Annual Report 2018-19, TV Licences for over-75s and Reality TV, HC 2432 Wednesday 17 July 2019. Ordered by the House of Commons to be published on 17 July 2019.
7. Rajeev Syall and agencies (27 March 2019) "Dominic Cummings found in contempt of parliament", Guardian
8. Julian Knight MP (19 January 2020), "BBC needs no holds barred review - and this is why", Daily Express
9. Adam Boulton (9 February 2020) "No. 10 is trying to control the media, and everyone in our democracy should be afraid" Sunday Times
10. Robert Shrimsley (14 February 2020) "Boris Johnson has backed Dominic Cummings over Sajid Javid — and there will be a cost" Financial Times Instant Insight

Chapter 19

Putting the National Interest First – Reimagining the BBC for its Second Century

A reformed and bigger BBC putting information engineering in the public interest at the centre of a new vision for the UK is in the national interest, argues the author of a volume of the corporation's official history, Jean Seaton

Number 10 says 'Out with the BBC licence fee! Off with its head!' as if it were a public enemy. It has apparently become an already settled issue. The licence fee needs re-imagining for the new information world. But 'abolishing' it without thought appears to be related to the will to tame the BBC. Part of an attempt to subordinate its separate power. Of course, destroying great complex things like the BBC is ridiculously easy. Like the 6th century Bamiyan Buddhas in Afghanistan or the 16th century Babri Masjid mosque in Ayodhya – once gone, they are indeed gone.

Do you want corrupt local government? Then sell off BBC local radio. Brexit has shown how communities suffer when they have no media to represent them to themselves or others. Without scrutiny local decisions will inevitably be captured by business interests. BBC local reporting is the last coherent public reporting force left locally, it ought to be grown. It needs to feed into the national agenda better. Lose it and you lose the local, the regional, and the power the corporation has to push issues up and down the political machine.

You want to diminish our role in the world to weaselly propaganda? Slash and burn the BBC but leave something called the World Service in place. The World Service ought to be bigger, it is vitally important in a news-impoverished world, where information is distorted by political interference, business interests and where journalists are attacked with impunity.

But without the mothership of values and force on the world's stage of an independent BBC, proud and sufficiently financed to back up its robust voice, the World Service could mutate into a government poodle. That will do us and the world no good at all.

A fit-for-purpose BBC

The mood around the BBC licence fee has shifted in the twinkling of an eye. To abolish the licence fee is to abolish the BBC and no one has actually wanted to do that before. For very good reasons. The full extent of this casually applied yet bizarre and dramatic turnaround is hardly appreciated in the storm of 'change' and dissolution we are in. We are all disrupters now. But beware what you wish for. Institutions like the BBC are very hard to build: they take long term, assiduous care. They are the product of the development and application of principles. In the case of the BBC, these were, first, protection of independent editorial judgement (the kind that made the BBC a world phenomenon during World War Two); second, impartiality so that everyone can be an informed citizen; third, imaginative boldness (the kind that made *Fawlty Towers*, *Fleabag*, *The Thick of it* and *Strictly*); and fourth, the accuracy and breadth of information and tone that made the World Service the station of the sound of freedom for audiences in the closed, un-free, world behind the walls of the Cold War. As we are right now in the middle of the third great war, one of information and cyber-attack we need a fit-for-purpose BBC as much as we did during the Blitz.

Good institutions – never perfect – keep us safe. Indeed, the independence of institutions creates a civilised and secure place for individuals and societies to flourish. In the case of the BBC it has created a public space of the mind for the nation and the world. Of course, change is good for institutions, they need to have a complex connection to the temper of the epoch. They have to reflect the times. But they are also there as an anchor to decency.

There have been previous arguments about the licence fee. A political sense that politicians never wanted to raise it when it was needed (except under John Birt's careful ministrations) but only when it suited their political agenda. A sense that poor people should not pay as much as rich. An ambiguity around what was in effect a hypothecated tax. All of this was allied to the fact that people like to moan about the BBC (in public), that the BBC made good copy, because people relate to it and it has 'celebrities' you can always take a pop at, and that a vast fabulously resourced lobbying industry has constantly attacked the corporation in their own interests. Politicians like to blame the BBC for being biased against them. Attacking the BBC has always been one way to knock other things off the front pages and somehow put politicians on the side of the 'public'.

Pious superiority

But the new attacks are different. Somewhere in the early 2000s, fuelled by social media, public life began to be conducted in terms of angry righteous indignation. It is a peculiar unrewarding form of discourse – which starts from the assumption of pious superiority. It developed a dangerous new nasty tone which had migrated from the tabloid press out into every day and social media. The BBC became the perpetual butt of this, and that added to the brew. Until now discussions of the licence fee and the BBC have also always had an element of ritual. Politicians would complain; yet in the end reality prevailed. The rational scrutiny of options and outcomes threw up the same conclusion time and time again, since the Peacock Report in 1984 – set up because Mrs Thatcher saw the licence fee as a tax – and repeatedly since then as committees and inquiries have explored alternative. They always came up with the same answer: if you wanted a BBC then you needed something like the licence fee.

What makes the current argument more surprising is that the BBC is *not* in the middle of any great scandal. Usually the attack on the BBC's funding is the consequence of another kind of row about BBC performance. Yes, equal pay was awkward, and took many people by surprise. But on the scale of BBC crises it was not major. Tony Hall took over during Savile affair and that was a beast of a crisis, for the first time putting the BBC at odds with audiences. Hall, a hugely decent and dedicated man, dealt with it compassionately and properly. He steadied the corporation, was adroit and clever, but straightforward not tricky, humane and a public servant.

With friends like these...

The alarming thing about this crisis is the weakness and inadequacy of the BBC's traditional constitutional protectors. Usually, despite the depredations of the Treasury, a key defender of the BBC in the last instance has been an impartial and rational civil service, whose members looked sideways at an institution whose core principles they understood. Can it still perform that role? And traditionally the Opposition, to whichever party is in power, has often been a key BBC defender. But we do not have a functioning opposition, and are unlikely to have one for years. Meanwhile the one-nation conservatives within the Conservative Party who have traditionally protected the BBC lost their seats in the strange election of 2019.

That the BBC does not know how to articulate its own defence is challenging. Not least perhaps it has a British sense of not wanting to recommend itself. Only outside observers can do that. So the BBC struggles internally and externally to find a voice to say what matters about it. Even able ex-politicians like James Purnell – for whom it might have come more easily – seem to fumble. Meanwhile the critics of the BBC (some dressed up as 'friends' who worry about 'our' BBC) range from those whose only claim to the public interest is their enduring, almost abstract hostility to the BBC, to the thoughtless and ignorant.

Put the BBC at the heart of a new vision for the UK

But it is also the case that the BBC argument cannot continue on the same merry-go-round. The case that it made for its first century no longer has purchase. It has to be shifted. The BBC not only faces a far more competitive market place than ever previously imagined with the vast media platforms dominating people's lives. It has – at every turn – to our collective and cultural disadvantage, been shorn of the capacity to engage with people where they now are. It proposed a 'public service' search engine and was prohibited from developing it by commercial concerns that it would compete too effectively. It proposed a video-on-demand service like Netflix , but was prohibited from developing it by commercial concerns that it would compete too effectively. At every turn narrow financial and competitive concerns have trumped the national interest. Now is the moment to change all of that.

The BBC used to be run by engineers who set the world's standards. We have never needed information engineers working in the public interest more. Make the BBC the hub of a new vision for the UK. All around the world people are worrying about how to manage the wild west of the internet. Well, we have the institution that with reform and inspiration could do something about it. We need to put the national, domestic and international interest first and create the possibility of a new BBC. You want to take back control? After getting Brexit done, what makes us more distinct, more ourselves? The BBC is your tool. Make it bigger, don't bully it. Trust it. The BBC is the always reformable institution that makes the public space of our national imaginations bigger and more generous. And that in the end is what Britain is.

About the contributor

Jean Seaton is Professor of Media History at the University of Westminster. Her expanded and updated volume of the official history of the BBC, *Pinkoes and Traitors: the BBC and the Nation 1974-87*, was published in 2016.

Chapter 20

Just how independent of government is the BBC?

Jane Martinson argues that the Johnson Government's thirst for controlling communication has made the role of director-general a poisoned chalice. The need to protect the corporation is, she says, urgent

The role of director-general is a poisoned chalice due to the Johnson Government's thirst for controlling communication, says Jane Martinson, and the need to protect the corporation is urgent

Over the past seven years, there has been one director-general of the BBC and eight culture secretaries. Oliver Dowden MP, the latest incumbent, can, at the very least, hope to attend one Wimbledon final before moving on from his cabinet post. But this time the new director-general may not get much longer.

The coming year will prove just how independent of government the BBC really is as it faces a series of huge challenges. Claire Enders tells me the conditions facing the BBC are the worst in her 35 years as a media analyst. "I wouldn't wish the DG job on my worst enemy."

Apocalyptic statements about its future have been made before, of course, but these challenges include a government that appears obsessed with, as a "senior Downing Street aide" told *The Sunday Times* in February, "whacking" the BBC, and a landscape that is undermining the principle of universal public service broadcasting.

Broadcasting by appointment

In January, Tony Hall announced he was stepping down as director-general of the BBC. In the first real test of the royal charter agreement – effectively the BBC's constitution – reached in 2016, chairman David Clementi gets to appoint Hall's replacement before his own four-year term runs out in February 2021.

Under the terms of the charter, the chairman himself is appointed by the government, which could mean that Clementi finds he isn't reappointed if his preferred candidate does not meet the approval of No 10. Support for the BBC director-general, both within and without, would normally protect the office holder from such overt political machinations. But these are not normal times.

Applications for the role of DG have to be in by 11 March, a month that coincides with the first letters warning over-75s that they will need to start paying their licence fees. By 1 April, responses are also due in to the review on decriminalising non-payment of the licence fee.

So, by this summer, the BBC faces the possibility of mass evasion by licence fee refuseniks (though the government is unlikely to change its mandatory status until 2027) and a slew of stories focused on the numbers of poor and unwell old people having to find £154.50 to watch the telly. This will provide great copy for the newspapers, which have for years waged war on the BBC for providing the news and entertainment they want to sell.

Fake news and unfair competition?

Make no mistake, the government's complaints against the BBC not only follow Trump's 'fake news' strategy – in which politicians realise they don't have to answer questions if they convince enough supporters all criticism is based on lies by a biased media – but also decades of complaint from the print media that the BBC creates unfair competition. It is a government, after all, led by a man who, for decades, worked for *The Telegraph*, owned by billionaires who make no secret of their dislike of taxation.

Witness the splash by Downing Street's favoured political editor, Tim Shipman, which trumpeted the government's plans to "change the face of British broadcasting", by chopping all but radios 3 and 4 and lots of TV stations too. But the print media has long blamed the BBC for its own woes, despite evidence that things are just as bad in countries with no state broadcaster. Read Nicky Morgan's piece in *The Daily Mail* in early 2020 in which she not only praised the paper for "shining the spotlight" on the "unfair and disproportionate" licence fee sanction, but compared the BBC with the defunct Blockbuster video chain, saying it needed to adapt to the modern streaming age. Furious BBC insiders retorted that when it first tried to launch a video-on-demand service (when Netflix was still pushing DVDs through letterboxes) the BBC was denied on competition grounds. "They tell us we've got to remain relevant and then when we try, they say we're killing commercial competition." She also pointed out that "more children now recognise the names Netflix and YouTube than they do the BBC", which is possibly true. She didn't point out that a premium streaming subscription of £144 a year only pays for entertainment, not the news or current affairs, or dedicated children's channels or BBC Bitesize or the World Service.

These priorities have long been known as the 'Rupert Murdoch agenda' after *The Sunday Times* boss's long-running complaints against the state broadcaster – hence the delight when it was reported that his daughter Elisabeth was considering a run at the DG job, which she denied. One report in the i newspaper called her a "compromise" candidate given the fact that Downing Street really wanted Rebekah Brooks, the head of Murdoch's UK print and radio business, to do the job.

Soft power, hard questions

Back to the very real challenges facing the BBC. Decriminalisation is a tricky issue for the BBC. Even though just five people went to prison for non-payment in 2018, that still feels like five too many. Yet, the whole output of the BBC – from *EastEnders* to Radio 3 – is based on the assumption that more or less everyone will pay. If those assumptions are unlikely to be held by young people who can't remember the last BBC programme they watched or listened to, then a debate needs to be had about what kind of BBC the UK needs.

The BBC fightback to date has consisted of David Clementi using a speech to highlight the threat to children's services and indeed the World Service, which costs some £240m a year. Making the argument that a UK out of the world's largest trading bloc may need all the soft power it can get, he said: "No other brand resonates around the world like the BBC... a diminished BBC is a weakened United Kingdom."

Other European countries either fund their public service broadcasters directly from government, or through a payroll tax on workers. Would this be any more satisfactory? Netflix-style subscriptions are mentioned all the time but somehow miss the technical challenges that you can't gate radio and television services when some 40 per cent of BBC-consuming homes use Freeview.

Dowden, who calls himself "the member of parliament for Albert Square" – because his constituency contains the Elstree studios where EastEnders, among many others, is filmed – was previously in charge of the "digital transformation" of government. He has been described as an "advocate of utilising technological solutions for public services". Which could be handy. Then again with John Whittingdale, who has argued for years that the licence fee is obsolete, back as a minister of state, perhaps Dowden will leave the BBC to him.

Whatever the government and its new culture minister decide, the BBC needs to work out not only how to adapt to digital technologies but also to build back the trust which has, for most of its history, protected it against political interference.

Hearts, minds and the control of communication

It may be a cliché but, in times of war, winning the battle for hearts and minds is more important than ever. And a nation as divided as the UK since the referendum has increasingly turned on its national broadcaster, despite polls that still say it is more trusted than any other news source.

The BBC is not perfect and needs to change but, faced with a government whose idea of taking back control seems to extend to the control of communication, the need to protect it is urgent. The next director-general could well be the last one that matters.

About the Contributor

Jane Martinson is the Marjorie Dean Professor of Financial Journalism at City University. She was previously head of media at *The Guardian* and is a former chair of Women in Journalism

Chapter 21

Dom's Dystopia 2027

John Mair peers into the future to discover that Dominic Cummings is Deputy Prime Minister in the third Johnson government. Cummings took up that role after the 2024 election when he won a seat in Sunderland. Here we have exclusive access to his blog from 2027

Well, Boris and I have finally sorted the BBC after eight years in office. We had it in mind from before day one but we had to go slowly at first to not *épater les bourgeoisie*. Things picked up later though once we were able to lever Lis Murdoch in as chair in 2021. She saw them through their last big beano, the Centenary Celebrations in 2022. Since then, it has been all uphill with the Bozo 'A' Team. Being a modest soul, let me list how we 'saved' the BBC.

Money

Firstly, we got rid of the insane idea of criminalising those who refused to pay the BBC licence fee/poll tax after a bit of softening up by Baroness Morgan in her short time as Culture Secretary (2019-2020).Then a quick three line Bill. The BBC said it would cost them £200 million per year in lost revenue. They were wrong. It is much more. People simply now regard the licence fee as voluntary. The BBC has lost £500million per year since 2021.

Then Bozo and I insisted that they kept their end of the Osborne bargain and give free TV licences to all over-75s.

Another quick three line Bill and the BBC was £750 million poorer. So, that's a cool one billion pound-plus bite out of their licence fee revenue. The nabobs of New Broadcasting House soon learned to cut their cloth. The cloth is now just £2bn licence fee per year and going south!

From next year, a Dom/Boris revolution, there will be just a £100 licence fee to cover BBC news and factual programmes. The rest of the jewels in the BBC crown will be on subscription on Britbox. We have stopped the corporation going the way of Blockbuster!

Services

George Osborne was right on this a decade or more ago. Wrong on Europe, right on the BBC. He said the corporation was simply trying to do too much. The reduced budget has seen to their imperial ambitions.

TELEVISION

BBC One and Two are still there (but see above re. factual only), BBC Three has come back on the terrestrial dial to attract the missing 'yoof'. BBC Four, though, has been folded into a night-time service on the BBC Two spectrum.

BBC (24 hour) News and BBC World News has been concertinaed to one service The number of presenters and producers cut in half. Programmes are now six hours long.

BBC iPlayer has been zizzed up – plenty more content up for longer windows, but you have to subscribe to watch it.

National and local regions: Only BBC Scotland survives since we won the IndyRef by a whisker in 2025. We need it to keep the Celts at bay. Wales and Northern Ireland broadcast in the early hours on BBC One.

Local TV: Down to five stations now – with just one half-hour programme a day in each mega-region.

RADIO

Radios 1 and 2 are still there but all output is sponsored just like Virgin Radio. No 'ad breaks' but a message at the top and bottom of each of the hours of the six in the programmes. There are no BBC Radio 1 Roadshows any more, nor any *Friday Night is Music Night* on Radio Two. Fripperies!

Radio 4 has been re-badged as Clever Talk Radio and Radio 5 Live as Radio Bloke. Both operate in reduced circs, cutting the cloth. BBC Radio 3 has been conflated with Scala Radio to make Scala Plus, and the BBC Proms have been set free as a profit-making company which they do with higher ticket prices.

The BBC Orchestras – national and regional – are simply no more.

Local Radio: For the nations and regions, see above. BBC Northern Ireland radio has joined its Protestant and Catholic stations in one. Likewise the local radio stations. Now in mega-regions just like 100 years ago.

BBC broadcast and engineering talent is now recruited via LinkedIn. No training is given.

BBC Sounds has been stopped from making original programmes. Podcasts and the like are left to the market, which is doing them very nicely.

BBC WORLD SERVICE

Severe cutbacks here. Only five or so tactical services have been retained for geo-political reasons. That list changes according to circumstances. World Service radio is part of post-Brexit Britain. It is now entirely financed by the Department for International Trade.

The number of foreign correspondents has been reduced to twenty in total. Essentially, they are regional firefighters used as and when, and paid by need. The era of Memsahib Tully has truly come to a close.

BBC SPORT

It is back in the market for live sport but to get it you have to use your BritBox sub. It means the corporation is once again feeding at the Premier League live trough. That is much reduced since Comcast pulled Sky out of football in 2022 citing "other priorities". Formula 1 is back at the BBC too – Sky walked away from that in 2023. The market went against those two big national sports.

BBC NEWS ONLINE

We think this is providing a good public service so have left it intact but commercial companies can now buy advertising space on the site.

BBC TECHNOLOGY

The great tech brains that help the BBC to keep ahead of the curve need to be preserved. So we have spun BBC Technology off to a separate profit-making and profit-sharing company.

STAFFING

When Boris and I walked into Number 10 there were 19,000 BBC staff but even they were unsure of the exact number. We've shaved that down to 10,000 today, less than a decade later. But the bone still has plenty on it.

SUMMARY

So, dear readers, you can see that in seven short years, the greatest PM since Churchill and I have well and truly 'sorted' the BBC.

About the contributor

Dominic Cummings MP is now Deputy Prime Minister. From 2019-2024 he was chief adviser and guru to Prime Minister Boris Johnson.

Bite-Sized Public Affairs Books are designed to provide insights and stimulating ideas that affect us all in, for example, journalism, social policy, education, government and politics.

They are deliberately short, easy to read, and authoritative books written by people who are either on the front line or who are informed observers. They are designed to stimulate discussion, thought and innovation in all areas of public affairs. They are all firmly based on personal experience and direct involvement and engagement.

The most successful people all share an ability to focus on what really matters, keeping things simple and understandable. When we are faced with a new challenge most of us need quick guidance on what matters most, from people who have been there before and who can show us where to start. As Stephen Covey famously said, "The main thing is to keep the main thing, the main thing."

But what exactly is the main thing?

Bite-Sized books were conceived to help answer precisely that question crisply and quickly and, of course, be engaging to read, written by people who are experienced and successful in their field.

The brief? Distil the 'main things' into a book that can be read by an intelligent non-expert comfortably in around 60 minutes. Make sure the book enables the reader with specific tools, ideas and plenty of examples drawn from real life. Be a virtual mentor.

We have avoided jargon – or explained it where we have used it as a shorthand – and made few assumptions about the reader, except that they are literate and numerate, involved in understanding social policy, and that they can adapt and use what we suggest to suit their own, individual purposes. Most of all the books are focused on understanding and exploiting the changes that we witness every day but which come at us in what seems an incoherent stream.

They can be read straight through at one easy sitting and then referred to as necessary – a trusted repository of hard-won experience.

Bite-Sized Books Catalogue

Bite-Sized Brexit Books

Caroline Stocks and John Mair
    Farmageddon? Brexit Book 5
        Brexit and British Agriculture
David Bailey, Alex De Ruyter, Neil Fowler and John Mair
    Carmageddon
        Brexit & Beyond for UK Auto
David Bailey, John Mair and Neil Fowler (Editors)
    Keeping the Wheels on the Road – Brexit Book 3
        UK Auto Post Brexit
Paul Davies, John Mair and Neil Fowler
    Will the Tory Party Ever Be the Same? – Brexit Book 4
        The Effect of Brexit
John Mair and Neil Fowler (Editors)
    Do They Mean Us – Brexit Book 1
        The Foreign Correspondents' View of the British Brexit
John Mair, Alex De Ruyter and Neil Fowler (Editors)
    The Case for Brexit – Brexit Book 2
John Mair and Steven McCabe, with Neil Fowler and Leslie Budd
    Brexit and Northern Ireland – Brexit Book 6
        Bordering on Confusion?

Business Books

Ian Benn
    Write to Win
        How to Produce Winning Proposals and RFP Responses
Matthew T Brown
    Understand Your Organisation
        An Introduction to Enterprise Architecture Modelling

Don Sharp
>   Nothing Happens Until You Sell Something
>>   A Personal View of Selling Techniques

Lifestyle Books

Anna Corthout
>   Alive Again
>>   My Journey to Recovery

Anna Corthout
>   Mijn Leven Herpakt
>>   Kruistocht naar herstel

Paul Davies – (Editor)
>   Still Crazy About George Eliot After 200 Years
>>   A Joyful Celebration of Her Works and Novels

Phil Davies
>   Don't Worry Be Happy
>>   A Personal Journey

Phil Davies
>   Feel the Fear and Pack Anyway
>>   Around the World in 284 Days

Stuart Haining
>   My Other Car is an Aston
>>   A Practical Guide to Ownership and Other Excuses to Quit
>>   Work and Start a Business

Bill Heine
>   Cancer – Living Behind Enemy Lines Without a Map

Regina Kerschbaumer
>   Yoga Coffee and a Glass of Wine
>>   A Yoga Journey

Gillian Perry
>   Capturing the Celestial Lights
>>   A Practical Guide to Imagining the Northern Lights

Arthur Worrell
>   A Grandfather's Story
>>   Arthur Worrell's War

Public Affairs Books

Eben Black
> Lies Lobbying and Lunch
>> PR, Public Affairs and Political Engagement – A Guide

John Mair and Richard Keeble (Editors)
> Investigative Journalism Today:
>> Speaking Truth to Power

John Mair, Richard Keeble and Farrukh Dhondy (Editors)
> V.S Naipaul:
>> The legacy

Christian Wolmar
> Wolmar for London
>> Creating a Grassroots Campaign in a Digital Age

John Mair and Neil Fowler (Editors)
> Do They Mean Us – Brexit Book 1
>> The Foreign Correspondents' View of the British Brexit

John Mair and Neil Fowler (Editors)
> Oil Dorado
>> Guyana's Black Gold

Sir John Redwood
> We Don't Believe You
>> Why Populists and the Establishment see the world differently

John Mills
> Economic Growth Post Brexit
>> How the UK should Take on the World

Fiction

Paul Davies
> The Ways We Live Now
>> Civil Service Corruption, Wilful Blindness, Commercial Fraud, and Personal Greed – a Novel of Our Times

Paul Davies
> Coming To
>> A Novel of Self-Realisation

Children's Books

Chris Reeve – illustrations by Mike Tingle

The Dictionary Boy

A Salutary Tale

Fredrik Payedar

The Spirit of Chaos

It Begins

Printed in Great Britain
by Amazon